AMERICA BEGINS AT HOME

THE WIFE & MOTHER GOD CALLS FOR THIS HOUR

Restoring the soul of a nation through the faith of her mothers.

WRITTEN AND COMPILED BY
JEN THOMPSON
CO-*FOUNDER OF SMORES AND STRIPES*
CO-*CREATOR OF THE UNDER GOD PROJECT*

Published by The Under God Project Press Dallas, Texas
© 2025 Jen Thompson. All rights reserved.

No portion of this publication may be reproduced or transmitted in any form or by any means without prior written permission of the publisher.

DEDICATION

FOR MY DAUGHTERS

THAT THEY MAY KNOW WHAT GOD EXPECTS OF THEM,
GROW IN GRACE AND TRUTH,
AND BECOME WOMEN WHOSE COURAGE AND FAITH
RESTORE THE HEART OF A HOME AND THE HONOR OF A NATION.

Mom

PREFACE

The Wife and Mother God Calls for This Hour

This book is written in the spirit of Titus 2, a sacred conversation between generations of women who refuse to forget God's design. It is not a manifesto of outrage but a revival of remembrance, a whisper from mother to daughter, saying, Come home to who you were created to be.

When Paul wrote to Titus, he charged older women to teach younger women "to be sober, to love their husbands, to love their children, to be discreet, chaste, keepers at home, good, obedient to their own husbands; that the word of God be not blasphemed" (Titus 2 : 4-5). These words were never meant to confine, but to preserve. They protect the sanctity of home and the testimony of the Gospel.

Today that testimony is under fierce attack. The enemy has turned his weapons toward women, the nurturers of nations and the stewards of faith. From the beginning he has sought to twist what God declared good, for "he is a liar, and the father of it" (John 8 : 44). If he can confuse the woman, he can confuse the world.

Our generation wrestles deeply with identity. Many are "ever learning, and never able to come to the knowledge of the truth" (2 Timothy 3 : 7). The culture teaches independence without reverence, confidence without surrender, and equality without holiness. Yet the peace of womanhood cannot be found in rebellion; it lives only in obedience to the Creator. The modern message claims that purity is oppression and submission is weakness, yet woman was created not as rival but as restorer, called to fill what man frames, to bring life where he builds. The heart of a nation is shaped not in halls of power but in the quiet rooms where women teach, heal, and refine. Every virtue recovered within her becomes a seed of revival without.

The modern message claims that purity is oppression and submission is weakness, but Scripture declares the opposite. "Whose adorning let it not be that outward adorning... but let it be the hidden man of the heart, in that which is not corruptible... of a meek and quiet spirit, which is in the sight of God of great price" (1 Peter 3 : 3-4). True beauty is not loud or boastful; it is born of the Spirit, not of self-promotion.

The wife and mother God calls for this hour, must learn to stand in truth with grace. She must be wise as serpents and harmless as doves (Matthew 10 : 16). Her strength is not in her voice but in her virtue. Her power is not in pride but in prayer. Every virtue in these pages confronts a counterfeit. Faithfulness answers convenience; purity silences corruption; cleanliness rebukes chaos; loyalty heals betrayal; reverence replaces arrogance. "Be not overcome of evil, but overcome evil with good" (Romans 12 : 21).

This book flows from the same heart as the Our Family Under God Compact; a call for women to reclaim covenant faith, beginning in the home. Each virtue is a stone in the altar of that covenant, laid by hand and heart for the generations that follow.

PREFACE

We have been called for such a time as this. As Esther stood before the king with courage and prayer, so must we stand before our generation with conviction and humility (Esther 4 : 14). The same Spirit who filled her heart now dwells in every woman who believes. The Lord has always raised women to restore what sin has broken. Deborah judged Israel with righteousness (Judges 4 : 4-5). Hannah prayed until her barrenness became blessing (1 Samuel 1 : 10-20). Mary surrendered with the words, "Behold the handmaid of the Lord; be it unto me according to thy word" (Luke 1 : 38). Their stories are not ancient relics but living examples of faith.

This book invites you to walk that same narrow way. "Stand ye in the ways, and see, and ask for the old paths, where is the good way, and walk therein, and ye shall find rest for your souls" (Jeremiah 6 : 16). Rest is not found in reinvention; it is found in returning.The world builds platforms that vanish; God builds homes that endure. "Except the Lord build the house, they labour in vain that build it" (Psalm 127 : 1). Every act of faithfulness within your home is a stone in a temple that cannot be shaken.

The call of Titus 2 belongs to every generation. Whether young or old, married or single, every woman who clings to Scripture becomes a teacher of good things. "Iron sharpeneth iron; so a man sharpeneth the countenance of his friend" (Proverbs 27 : 17). When women live God's truth, they sharpen the faith of all who see them. This is why the enemy labors to make women despise their role. He fears the power of a praying mother and the steadfastness of a faithful wife. "For the weapons of our warfare are not carnal, but mighty through God to the pulling down of strong holds" (2 Corinthians 10 : 4). A woman walking in obedience is a weapon in God's hand.

Let these words become your armor and your peace. Take every virtue as a banner and every verse as a promise. "Strength and honour are her clothing; and she shall rejoice in time to come" (Proverbs 31 : 25). You were never meant to hide in fear, but to shine as light in a darkened world.

Sister, this is our Titus 2 moment. Together we rise as daughters of truth in an age of deception. We will rebuild the walls of womanhood with faith, hope, and charity. "Watch ye, stand fast in the faith, quit you like men, be strong. Let all your things be done with charity" (1 Corinthians 16 : 13-14).

May we become the wives and mothers God needs us to be: faithful in heart, pure in spirit, courageous in calling, and radiant with the glory of Christ our Lord.

Welcome to the front lines of grace.
Welcome to **The Wife & Mother God Calls For This Hour**

The Wife and Mother God Calls for This Hour

GOD MAKES FAMILIES

From the very beginning, God's design for nations began with families.

He did not start with armies, governments, or kings—He started with homes.

When the floodwaters receded, Noah stepped out of the ark and built an altar to the Lord, dedicating his family and the generations that would follow.

When the world turned to idolatry, Abraham was called out of Ur to become the father of nations, through faith and obedience. When bondage held God's people captive, Moses led them out of Egypt—not as scattered individuals, but as tribes and households—families under God. When the promise passed to Isaac and Jacob, God renewed His covenant through generations, reminding them that their children and their children's children would bear His name.

God has always built nations through the faith of families.

Centuries later, that same truth echoes in America.

FAMILIES UNDER GOD MAKE AMERICA

In 1954, President Dwight D. Eisenhower added the words "Under God" to the pledge of allegiance and signed it into law, affirming that our liberty comes not from government, but from our Creator. He did that because for the upcoming six years American families had been doing that on thier own.

In 1948, Louis Albert Bowman, a humble father out of Chicago, first added "under God" to the Pledge of Allegiance at his church and family gatherings. Looking out at a world on the brink of war again, he was inspired by Abraham Lincoln's timeless words from 1863—that "this nation, under God, shall have a new birth of freedom."

Lincoln's phrase at Gettysburg was not in his prepared notes. He spoke it under conviction, echoing the divine truth proclaimed by the Founders in 1776—that all men are created equal and endowed by their Creator with certain unalienable rights: life, liberty, and the pursuit of happiness.

And those Founders, in turn, stood on the shoulders of those who came before them. In 1620, my great-grandfather William Brewster helped pen the Mayflower Compact— the first governing document of this land. It was not written by prophet, pastor, president, or king, but by families. Families who knelt before God and declared that their colony would exist "for the glory of God and the advancement of the Christian faith."

FAMILIES MAKE NATIONS
THE COVENANT CONTINUES

From the Ark to the Mayflower, from Plymouth Rock to the halls of Congress, the story is the same: when families remember God, nations are preserved; when families forget Him, nations fall.

Every generation must renew this covenant in its own time. Each must invite God back into our homes, our schools, and our national identity—starting with our families.

And so we return to Joshua, standing at Shechem after the battles were won. He called the people together, placed a great stone beneath the oak tree, and declared before all Israel:

"As for me and my house, we will serve the Lord." — JOSHUA 24:15

That stone stood as a witness to their covenant—a physical reminder that nations rise or fall on the faith of their families.

Today, this Compact is that stone. This is our covenant.

A LIVING COVENANT BETWEEN FAMILIES

Every Family Under God Compact is hand-pressed on archival paper, designed to last for generations. Each family signs their name, sealing their promise as a household that will serve the Lord. (See us at UnderGodProject.com or one of our national events.)

Families across the nation create their own family seals with the seal-making kit included in each Compact—a wax seal bearing the words One Nation Under God. It is a symbol that their family is ordained and created by God.

Each family signs and seals their Compact. Many send their finished seals back to be shared, and we include these signed wax seals in future Compact kits—so that every new family receives a piece of another family's covenant, a tangible reminder that we are truly One Family Under God.

Just as the Mayflower Compact united families in a common promise, this covenant binds today's families together in a shared faith and destiny. It is a call to restoration—of home, of heritage, and of hope.

THE WIFE AND MOTHER GOD CALLS FOR THIS HOUR

AN AMERICAN FAMILY PROMISE

OUR FAMILY UNDER GOD

A Promise

We are the {...} family, and on this {...} day of {Month}, of, {year} we declare that we are One Family Under God.

We believe that it is our right and our privilege to glorify God, and to enjoy and give thanks for what He has given us, especially for one another. The story of our faith is a story of the creation, sanctification, and preservation of families, and the story of our family is a continuation of the divine story.

We believe that God created families, and therefore the family is sacred and ordained by God. We believe that our family was created specifically for this time.

We know that every father and mother before us has led directly to our family today, and we believe they have been placed in our history so that we could be brought together.

As a family we pledge to love one another, to be a light to each other and the world around us. We pledge to learn more about our family history, and to learn and instruct our children on how best to honor God with our time, our talents, and our treasures.

As parents, we believe that our children are a gift from God, and our highest responsibility on earth.

As children, we believe that we are given the opportunity to learn from our fathers and mothers, and theirs before them, how to live an abundant and fulfilling life by honoring God and our parents.

We believe we are always essential to each other, essential to God's family, our extended family on earth.

We know that though there may be prodigals, or in pain, or wandering for a time, and while some of us may have been lost, we are still a family created by God. All of us were once prodigals to God, yet never abandoned or lost to Him, so we commit to never abandon those he has given to us.

We pledge to strengthen our faith and family ties, to uplift and encourage one another, and to stand firm in the face of any effort within or without to dim our light, love, or liberty to one another.

To that end we promise together as a family to continually: {personal family promises}

May God give us patience, strength, and peace as we keep these promises to one another, and may

God bless
THIS AMERICAN FAMILY.
In the Name of God,
Amen.

YOUR FAMILY HISTORY

America is the courage that crossed the ocean, the faith that built churches and schools, the sacrifice that tilled the soil and defended freedom—all of it lives on through families. Your family history is American history.

The same grit that settled the frontier, the same devotion that knelt in prayer at Valley Forge, the same ingenuity that built railroads, wrote hymns, and raised flags on distant shores—all of it runs through your veins. You are part of the great tapestry of God's providence woven through this nation.

When you discover your ancestors, you don't just find names and dates—you find identity. Stories of faith, hardship, and triumph. You begin to see that you are not here by chance. God has been faithful to your family from the beginning—and He will be faithful still.

"KNOW therefore that the Lord thy God, He is God, the faithful God, who keeps covenant and mercy with them that love Him and keep His commandments to a thousand generations."

—DEUTERONOMY 7:9

How to Begin

You don't need to be a historian to begin this journey. Just a willing heart.

1. Create a FamilySearch Account
    Visit FamilySearch.org
    Click "Create Account."
    Enter your name, birth date, and email address.
    Choose a password and confirm your account through the email they send.

Once logged in, you'll have access to billions of historical records and family trees—all free of charge.

2. Add What You Know
    Start with yourself, your parents, and your grandparents.
    Add birthplaces, marriage dates, and photos if you have them.
    Each name you add strengthens the bridge between your story and history.

IS AMERICAN HISTORY

3. Find Your Heroes

Each hero in this book includes a Family History ID (FHID) from FamilySearch. Enter the ID into the search bar at FamilySearch to view that hero's family line. Click "View Relationship" to see if and how you are connected.

You may find that your ancestor fought for liberty, built a homestead, or signed a document that changed history. Whether your connection is close or distant, it reminds you that their story and your story are threads in the same divine design.

4. Join the National Garden Group Hosted by Under God Project

Visit RelativeFinder.org
Log in using your FamilySearch account
Select "Groups" "Join Group"
Enter Group Name: National Garden of American Heroes
Enter Password: UGP1776

Inside the group, you'll see which of the 250 National Garden Heroes you're related to—and how. Each connection is a reminder that the same faith, courage, and virtue that shaped this nation still live in your bloodline.

Carry the Legacy

Record what you find. Tell the stories. Add photos, journal entries, and memories in these pages. Your family's story deserves to be preserved. The heroes who built America didn't see themselves as famous—they saw themselves as faithful. They lived ordinary lives with extraordinary virtue. Their stories now call you to remember who you are, where you come from, and Who holds your future.

In their courage, find your own.
In their faith, strengthen yours.
In their legacy, continue the story.

For the same God who guided them still guides you.

"Look unto the rock whence ye are hewn, and to the hole of the pit whence ye are digged. Look unto Abraham your father, and unto Sarah that bare you."
—ISAIAH 51:1–2

LET'S BEGIN

"...And who knows whether you have not come to the kingdom for such a time as this?"

ESTHER 4:14

THE WIFE AND MOTHER GOD CALLS FOR THIS HOUR

A PRAYER TO BEGIN

Heavenly Father,

   We come before Thee with humble hearts and open hands. Thank Thee for creating us in Thine image and calling us to walk as women of virtue, grace, and light. Cleanse our hearts, renew our minds, and fill our homes with Thy peace.
   "Create in me a clean heart, O God; and renew a right spirit within me" (Psalm 51 : 10).

Lord, teach us to love our husbands, cherish our children, and build our homes upon Thee. Help us to cast down every lie that tells us we are not enough, for Thy Word declares, "Ye are complete in Him" (Colossians 2 : 10). Holy Spirit, breathe upon these pages; let every word convict and comfort, correct and confirm. Open our eyes to see the beauty of obedience and the strength of gentleness.

 "Thy word is a lamp unto my feet, and a light unto my path" (Psalm 119 : 105). Make our homes sanctuaries where Thy presence abides. Let kindness rule our tongues, peace our hearts, and joy our countenances. May our eyes be honest, our words seasoned with grace, our posture at peace. As men guard, let us give; as they build, let us fill. Bless the work of our hands that every meal and moment may bring Thee praise.

Forgive us for doubting Thy design and seeking approval apart from Thee. Restore the joy of our salvation and uphold us with Thy free Spirit (Psalm 51 : 12). Strengthen every weary mother and steady every uncertain wife. Let each woman know she was chosen for this season and placed in this generation by Thy divine hand. "For we are His workmanship, created in Christ Jesus unto good works" (Ephesians 2 : 10).
Grant us courage to live as lights in the darkness, to call good what Thou hast called good, and holy what Thou hast called holy. Let our lives declare, "As for me and my house, we will serve the Lord" (Joshua 24 : 15).

Father, we dedicate this journey to Thee. Let these lessons and our obedience bring glory to Thy name, and may their fruit bless generations yet unborn.`

In the sacred Name of Jesus Christ, Amen.

MY COVENANT OF BIBLICAL WOMANHOOD

A DECLARATION FOR THE JOURNEY AHEAD

I, a daughter of the Most High God, enter this covenant with humility and faith.

I was created in His image, female by divine design, and chosen for such a time as this (Genesis 1 : 27; Esther 4 : 14).
 His Word is truth and the standard of my life (Psalm 119 : 160).
I lay down the false identities of this world and take up the cross of Christ (Luke 9 : 23). I choose faithfulness when it is easier to flee, wisdom when the world speaks folly, and purity when culture celebrates corruption.
 I will be clean in body and home, gentle in speech, loyal in love, and reverent in spirit, "that the word of God be not blasphemed" (Titus 2 : 5).
I will carry myself with grace and refinement, knowing that beauty and poise are testimonies of Thy order and love. As men guard, I will give; as they build, I will fill. Bless the work of my hands that my home may be a living sanctuary where Thy presence abides. When I am weary, I will pray; when I am afraid, I will sing; when the world demands I bow, I will stand. "For God hath not given us the spirit of fear; but of power, and of love, and of a sound mind" (2 Timothy 1 : 7).

I will honor the women before me and teach those who come after me, "that they may teach the young women to be sober, to love their husbands, to love their children" (Titus 2 : 4). I will adorn myself not with vanity but with virtue, for "the ornament of a meek and quiet spirit... is in the sight of God of great price" (1 Peter 3 : 4). My worth is not defined by culture but by the God who calls me beloved (Ephesians 1 : 6). "She is clothed with strength and honour; and she shall rejoice in time to come" (Proverbs 31 : 25). When I falter, I will rise; when I fail, I will repent; when I fear, I will remember His mercy endureth forever (Psalm 136 : 1). Today I covenant to live as a woman under God—faithful, wise, pure, loyal, and steadfast.
 May this vow mark the beginning of a new chapter written by grace, guided by truth, and sealed by the Spirit.

In signing this, I prepare my heart to join my household in a greater vow — to live as a family under God, that our lineage may bear the mark of His covenant for generations to come.

In all things, I will strive to be The Wife & Mother God Calls This Hour
So help me, Lord Jesus Christ.

Signature: _____
Date: _____

The Wife and Mother God Calls for This Hour

PHASES OF BIBLICAL WOMANHOOD

A MAP OF BECOMING; FROM INNOCENCE TO LEGACY

A woman's life unfolds in seasons, each one holy and appointed by God. From innocence to legacy, her journey is a tapestry of grace, virtue, and divine purpose.

In the earliest years, from **birth to twelve**,

she dwells in a season of wonder and affection when her heart learns by example and her spirit opens easily to goodness. Here she discovers joy, obedience, and curiosity, learning to trust and to love as a child of God. "Let the little children come to Me."

From **twelve to eighteen**

she enters when discipline, learning, and spiritual awareness begin to take root. She grows in diligence, humility, and respect, seeking wisdom that will guide her choices. This is when she learns who she is and whose she is; "Train up a child in the way he should go."

Between **eighteen and twenty-four**

comes the beautiful awakening of purpose. She begins to refine both her inner and outer beauty through service, study, and faith. This is the season of becoming—learning grace, faith, excellence, and discipline, setting the course of her womanhood under God's hand. "Let the beauty of the Lord be upon us."

From **twenty-five to forty**

she lives the fruitful season of where love deepens into labor and devotion becomes creation. Whether through bearing children or shaping hearts within her home, she builds a sanctuary of order and warmth, teaching, discipling, and strengthening those entrusted to her care. She learns sacrifice and tenderness; she becomes the keeper of peace. "She looks well to the ways of her household."

Between **forty and fifty-five**

her life enterswhen the seeds she planted begin to bloom in the lives of others. Her home and children reflect her labor, and she now turns outward in mentorship and guidance. This is the season of wisdom, gentleness, and discernment, when strength and dignity become her clothing and peace her testimony.

Beyond fifty-five

she walks in the sacred calling of the matriarch. Her hands have built, her prayers have sustained, and now her voice becomes counsel to generations. In faithfulness and humility she teaches younger women to love well, live reverently, and walk in gratitude before the Lord. Her courage steadies families and her wisdom anchors homes; "Teach the younger women to be sober, to love their husbands, to love their children."

Each phase is a chapter in the same holy story; a woman becoming who God designed her to be. Every season carries its own beauty and burden, yet all lead her toward eternal purpose. Ask yourself, which season am I in, and how is God shaping me for the next?

TABLE OF CONTENTS

DEDICATION 3
PREFACE 5
LET'S BEGIN 15
PART I 23
FOUNDATIONS OF GODLY WOMANHOOD 23
CHAPTER 1 25
CHAPTER 2 35
CHAPTER 3 45
CHAPTER 4 55
CHAPTER 5 65
CHAPTER 6 75
CHAPTER 7 85
PART II 95
CHAPTER 8 97
CHAPTER 9 107
CHAPTER 10 117
CHAPTER 11 127
CHAPTER 12 137
PART III..147
CHAPTER 13 149
CHAPTER 14 159
CHAPTER 15 169

CHAPTER 16	179
CHAPTER 17	189
CHAPTER 18	199
PART IV	209
CHAPTER 19	211
CHAPTER 20	221
CHAPTER 21	231
CHAPTER 22	241
CHAPTER 23	251
CHAPTER 24	261
PART V	271
CHAPTER 25	273
CHAPTER 26	283
CHAPTER 27	293
CHAPTER 28	303
CHAPTER 29	313
From Generation to Generation	323

PART I

FOUNDATIONS OF GODLY WOMANHOOD

"WE BELIEVE THAT GOD CREATED FAMILIES, AND THEREFORE THE FAMILY IS SACRED AND ORDAINED BY GOD"
-OUR FAMILY UNDER GOD COMPACT

CHAPTER 1

THE WAR ON WOMANHOOD

*"*STAND *ye in the ways, and see, and ask for the old paths, where is the good way, and walk therein, and ye shall find rest for your souls." Jeremiah 6 : 16*

THE WAR ON WOMANHOOD

From the beginning, the enemy fixed his aim upon the woman because she carries the image of life and the power to shape hearts. If he can confuse the woman, he can confuse the world. The battle is not against flesh and blood but against the lies that twist what God called good. The assault is steady and cunning. It questions design, mocks purity, and belittles the covenant.

God created woman to receive and to refine. Man frames and guards; woman fills and gives form. Families flourish when this order is honored. Homes become sanctuaries when grace governs their rooms. The enemy hates sanctuaries. He wages war by emptying homes of holiness and filling minds with noise.

The woman who remembers her design becomes dangerous to darkness. She heals what sin has fractured and rebuilds what pride has torn down. Her obedience repairs generations because it points hearts back to the Creator's pattern.

The Tactics of the Age

The spirit of the age praises independence without reverence, sells confidence without surrender, and offers equality without holiness. The result is restlessness that never finds rest. Many learn endlessly yet never come to the knowledge of truth. The world calls meekness weakness and purity oppression.; but scripture calls meekness precious and purity beautiful.

The assault also comes through disorder. When the home loses rhythm, peace begins to fade. When promises are broken, trust dissolves. When words grow careless, love is wounded. The enemy rarely shouts; he whispers. He persuades the weary mother that her work is unseen and unworthy. He tempts the young woman to measure her worth by attention instead of virtue.

This is the quiet war that wages in every heart: the battle between pride and purpose, between self and surrender. The woman who sees it clearly can no longer live carelessly. She begins to fight not with anger but with awareness.

The assault on womanhood is not merely social; it is spiritual. Every attack on marriage, motherhood, and modesty strikes at the very heart of covenant. The enemy knows that if he can dissolve the covenant in the home, he can unravel a nation.

Covenant has always been the heart of womanhood. From Eve's first promise to Mary's "Be it unto me," every generation is invited to renew it. To live under God is to dwell within that promise; to bring order where the world breeds confusion, to cradle light in a culture that worships shadow. The battle for womanhood is not won by rebellion, but by return—by remembering what was holy from the beginning.

God's Design Restated

Scripture reveals the antidote. Paul charged the older women to teach the younger women to love their husbands and children, to be discreet and chaste, to manage their households with goodness, so that the Word of God would not be blasphemed. This instruction was never meant to confine. It was meant to preserve. It guards the testimony of the Gospel and protects the peace of the house. This is the pattern of covenant lived in daily form. The sacred trust of womanhood under God, where faith is not only professed, but practiced.

The design is not rivalry; it is harmony. As men guard, women give. As men raise the walls, women fill them with warmth and light. Within that order lies beauty and freedom. When the design is honored, children learn security, marriages grow strong, and generations inherit stability. Every home that honors this design becomes a living covenant, a place where the promises of God take root and bear fruit across generations.

To restore womanhood is to restore worship. Each act of obedience reclaims territory from confusion. Every meal served in love and every truth spoken in grace rebuilds what the world has tried to erase. This is how covenant is renewed; not in grand gestures, but in the quiet consistency of faith made visible.

How We Stand and How We Fight

We do not fight people. We resist lies with truth and overcome evil with good. Our weapons are not of flesh but of faith. They pull down strongholds of deception and raise up banners of light. We answer convenience with faithfulness, corruption with purity, chaos with order, betrayal with loyalty, and pride with reverence. Through these virtues the covenant is defended, and through them the home remains under God.

Prayer becomes our lifeline. Scripture becomes our standard. Gratitude becomes our guard against bitterness. Service becomes our joy. Repentance becomes our return to peace. Through these simple and sacred acts, the woman of God wages her quiet war with victory already promised. The world may not applaud her battles, but heaven records every one. God sees the faithfulness that no one else notices. He honors the mother who prays, the daughter who obeys, and the wife who stands firm in love.

A Call to Rise

This is our moment. We refuse the counterfeit and return to the good and ancient paths. We choose reverence over arrogance and wisdom over impulse. We choose to be women under God; faithful, wise, pure, and steadfast. In doing so, we renew the promise of our homes and restore the foundation of our nation. Every unseen act of obedience is seen by heaven and sows peace for generations yet to come.

The pages that follow will clothe this calling in daily life. We begin with Faithfulness, for steadfast love under God supports every other virtue. Before a woman can rebuild her home, she must be anchored in promise. That promise is the quiet vow to live under God; faithful in heart, steadfast in hope, and surrendered in purpose. That is where our journey begins.

THE WIFE AND MOTHER GOD CALLS FOR THIS HOUR
FROM MY HEARTH

I first began to see the war on womanhood when the world's definition of strength started to sound nothing like God's. Everywhere I turned, women were being told that worth could only be proven through striving; through climbing ladders, claiming titles, and competing with men. "Equality" became the banner, but the cost was quiet joy. It was as if peace, gentleness, and devotion had been rebranded as weakness.

I watched as voices around me insisted that women should fill every role, not because they were called or prepared, but because they wanted to prove they could. What began as a quest for dignity turned into a denial of design. The message was loud: Be everything but what God made you to be.
The more I listened, the more I realized the world was offering a counterfeit. Its version of freedom required rebellion; its version of fulfillment demanded pride. But the longer I walked with God, the clearer His truth became. Womanhood was never a limitation; it was a holy calling.

From the beginning, God saw that it was not good for man to be alone. When He formed woman, creation was finally complete, and for the first time He called it very good. We were not made to compete with men but to complete the work of God beside them. He designed us as counterparts—two halves of one mission; to bring forth life, to nurture what is good, and to create harmony that reflects the peace of heaven.

That conviction took root early in me. I grew up wanting to honor God in every choice, what I said, what I wore, how I treated others. In school, that made me different. I didn't drink or curse or follow the crowd. I wanted my life to please the One who gave it. Some people didn't understand. A few laughed quietly, others teased openly, and many simply looked at me as if I belonged to another time.

Standing for purity in a culture that prizes attention can feel lonely. But I learned early that conviction will always cost comfort. There were gatherings I wasn't invited to, jokes whispered when I walked by, and moments when my faith was tested by those who said I was missing out. Yet even in those small hurts, God was teaching me endurance. He was forming in me a quiet courage, the kind that doesn't need to prove itself, only to remain faithful.

When boys I dated pressured me to cross lines I had promised not to, I had to decide whose voice I would honor, God's or theirs. I chose God's. Saving intimacy for marriage wasn't easy in a world that calls purity outdated, but obedience became my peace. Each time I said no to compromise, I was saying yes to something higher: trust in God's plan and reverence for His design.

THE BATTLE WITHIN

In those years, I discovered that purity isn't pride, it's worship. It's saying, "Lord, You can trust me with the body You made and the future You are writing." The world celebrates self-expression; Scripture calls us to self-control. One promises pleasure; the other produces peace. And as my faith deepened, so did my freedom. The pressure to be accepted by everyone lifted. I began to care less about being liked and more about being led. Yet I've learned that this battle doesn't end when youth fades; it only changes form.

Even in adulthood, the pressure to please can be relentless. There are times I have felt the quiet tug to fold; to soften truth for the comfort of others, to bend conviction for the sake of keeping peace, to say yes when my spirit knew God was asking me to stand still. Whether it's a family expectation, a friendship strained by boundaries, or the subtle guilt that comes when obedience looks like distance, I have had to choose between comfort and calling.

The Lord has reminded me again and again that love without truth is not love at all. Being gracious does not mean being silent, and being kind does not mean being compliant. Obedience to God will sometimes disappoint people I care about, but disobedience to Him will always wound my own soul. I am learning that peace is not found in the absence of conflict but in the presence of conviction. True harmony comes when I live the life He directs, not the one others desire for me.

And so I walk this narrow road with greater resolve. I still stumble, still learn, still long to do it all with gentleness, but I no longer confuse gentleness with surrender. That's when I understood the true battlefield; the war was not just around me; it was after me. It was after every daughter who might one day raise her children to love the Lord. The enemy's first lie to Eve is still the one he whispers now: "God is holding out on you." But what the world calls liberation, Heaven calls loss.

To be a woman under God is not to shrink; it is to shine differently. It is to stand as a restorer in a world of rebellion, to choose faithfulness when faithlessness feels easier, to bring life where others tear down. I have learned that courage isn't loud; it's quiet. It's the confidence of a woman who refuses to be redefined. My strength is not in my defiance but in my devotion. My victory is not in proving the world wrong, but in proving God faithful.

Every generation must choose its allegiance, to the clamor of culture or the call of Christ. I have chosen mine. And when my daughters one day face the same battle, I pray they too will remember that womanhood was never a wound to heal, but a wonder to honor. The war on womanhood does not begin in politics or headlines; it begins in the heart.

Every generation faces the same deception that first entered the garden, the question that still echoes through time: "Hath God said?" (Genesis 3:1). It is the ancient temptation to redefine what God has already called good. When we surrender His design for the comfort of approval, the battle is lost before it ever reaches the world around us. But when a woman chooses truth over ease, she becomes a defender of sacred order. Her obedience pushes back the darkness not by might, but by meekness.

God does not call His daughters to be loud in resistance, but steadfast in reverence. The victory begins not in argument, but in alignment; when a woman's heart, home, and habits return to the Word that shaped her. This is the foundation of restoration: to remember that womanhood was never meant to be reinvented, only redeemed.

Reflection Questions

Where have I unknowingly exchanged God's design for the world's expectations?

Which tactic of the age most unsettles my peace, and how can I answer it with Scripture?

How might my obedience renew the promise within my home and strengthen the generations after me?

What first small act of obedience can restore order and hope in my home today?

Prayer of Resolve
Father of Truth,

Open my eyes to the lies that have shaped my thinking. Anchor my heart in Thy Word and restore honor to my home. Renew within me the covenant of grace that binds my family to Thee.

Make me a woman who resists deception with faith, who rebuilds what the enemy has broken, and who walks daily in the beauty of Thy design.

Strengthen me to guard what is holy, to serve with joy, and to love without fear.

In the name of Jesus Christ, Amen.

CHAPTER 2

Faithfulness Steadfast Love As Covenant; Endurance Over Emotion

"O Lord, Thou art my God; I will exalt Thee, I will praise Thy name; for Thou hast done wonderful things, Thy counsels of old are faithfulness and truth." — Isaiah 25 : 1

Faithfulness is the first stone in the foundation of womanhood because every other virtue depends upon it. To be faithful is to remain when it would be easier to leave, to serve when no one notices, and to believe when sight has faded. It is not a fleeting emotion but a resolve that deepens through seasons of testing. Steadfastness anchors the heart when life pulls in uncertain directions. It holds the line between what is promised and what is lived, between the word spoken and the deed fulfilled.

In a world that prizes constant reinvention, steadfastness may appear ordinary, yet heaven calls it holy. The woman who stays the course is rare because her devotion is born from covenant, not convenience. Her constancy becomes the first fulfilment of the family's promise before God.

Her love matures through pressure, her peace is forged in patience, and her endurance becomes a living testimony of God's faithfulness. She does not drift with circumstance but rests upon Scripture, trusting that His promises remain sure.

Each morning, she renews her quiet vow to walk in grace and obedience. Her household may never witness the prayers she prays before sunrise or the forgiveness she offers before resentment can root itself. Those hidden acts of loyalty become the mortar of her family's strength. Her steadfastness sets the rhythm of the home, a peace that reminds all who enter that God is unchanging and near.

Faithfulness in Marriage

To be a faithful wife is more than avoiding betrayal; it is guarding a sacred covenant sealed before God. The vows exchanged at the altar are not fragile words of romance but eternal promises of endurance and trust.

When disappointment arises, she does not measure her love by ease but by faith. Her steadfastness becomes the vessel through which grace continues to flow.

Marriage is not sustained by constant passion but by consistent prayer. A faithful wife learns that unity grows when she chooses peace over pride and forgiveness over frustration. When she feels unseen, she turns first to the Lord, whose eyes never turn away. Her devotion mirrors Christ's love for His church: steadfast, forgiving, and enduring.

Her husband may not always voice it, but her steadfast spirit grants him courage. The world can be loud and hostile, yet he returns home to calm. He may lead with strength, but she steadies the household with grace. In that divine partnership, they reflect God's own order. Their covenant becomes a testimony that faith kept in the smallest things holds nations together. Her faithfulness does not make her silent; it makes her strong enough to stand when the wind rises.

Faithfulness in Motherhood

A mother's steadfastness is the first glimpse of God's nature her children will ever know. When she keeps her word, comforts their fears, and forgives freely, they begin to understand that love endures. Her tone, her rhythm, her gentle routines; all teach that security is born from constancy.

In her presence they learn that God can be trusted because love remains even when they fail. The long hours of motherhood are a sacred classroom. Every meal prepared, every prayer whispered, every correction offered in gentleness

plants seeds of faith. Her consistency teaches that obedience and affection are not enemies but companions. Even when exhaustion settles, she chooses gratitude, trusting that her unseen work is seen by God.

On weary days she remembers that heaven measures not her perfection but her perseverance. Each act of care becomes a form of worship. Her constancy, though unseen, mirrors the endurance of the Lord Himself, who never slumbers nor forgets His own.

Faithfulness in Sisterhood

Steadfast women bring stability to every circle they touch. In friendship they guard confidence, speak truth with kindness, and remain loyal when others drift away. Their reliability is a quiet ministry. When they say yes, they follow through. When they promise prayer, they truly pray. People find rest in their word because it mirrors the faithfulness of God.

In an age where relationships often bend under pressure, steadfastness within the sisterhood stands out as courage. A faithful woman listens before speaking and blesses rather than broadcasts. She does not seek attention but seeks to strengthen others. Her presence invites peace because she has learned that love is not proven by emotion but by endurance.

Her consistency within the sisterhood gives weight to her witness. When she serves, she serves cheerfully; when she gives, she gives sincerely. Her life becomes a sermon that requires no pulpit. Through steadfast love she adorns the Gospel, showing that the grace which saves also sustains.

Faithfulness Toward God

Steadfastness toward God is the wellspring of all other faithfulness. It is not born from willpower but from worship. It grows in the secret place, watered by prayer and strengthened through trial. When the heavens seem silent, the faithful woman keeps singing. When her plans crumble, she keeps trusting. Her eyes remain fixed on the One who never changes.

To be steadfast before God is to believe that His timing is perfect, even when it feels delayed. It is to obey when no reward appears and to rest in His promises when circumstances say otherwise. Such faith is not passive; it is active endurance rooted in love. She clings to Scripture as to a lifeline, knowing that the same God who began a good work in her will complete it.

When fear whispers that she is forgotten, she remembers

His word: "The steadfast love of the Lord never ceases; His mercies never come to an end" (Lamentations 3 22). That truth steadies her heart. It becomes her anthem and her armor. Faithfulness toward God renews the covenant of her soul and becomes the promise her family inherits. From it flows every act of loyalty, every word of grace, and every choice to remain when others retreat.

Faithfulness steadies the heart; righteousness directs its steps. The woman who learns to remain steadfast now learns to stand upright, for steadfast love becomes the soil where holy courage grows

THE WIFE AND MOTHER GOD CALLS FOR THIS HOUR

HANNAH

"For this child I prayed; and the Lord hath given me my petition which I asked of Him."
— 1 Samuel 1 : 27

Hannah's story begins in silence. The ache of unanswered prayer had settled deep within her, like dust upon a long-forgotten altar. Year after year she journeyed to the house of the Lord, watching other women cradle what she longed to hold. Her rival mocked her barrenness. Her husband tried to comfort her with words that could not reach the wound. Yet Hannah's grief did not turn her bitter; it turned her heavenward.

When words failed, her lips still moved. Scripture says she was "in bitterness of soul, and prayed unto the Lord, and wept sore." That is where prayer begins, not in eloquence but in honesty. She poured out her heart until her pain became prayer, and her prayer became worship. Even when the priest misunderstood her tears, accusing her of drunkenness, she did not defend herself with pride. She answered softly, "No, my lord, I am a woman of a sorrowful spirit." Her humility became her defense; her sincerity, her strength.

In that sacred moment, her supplication became surrender. She no longer prayed only for a son; she prayed for a purpose. "If Thou wilt give unto Thine handmaid a man child, then I will give him unto the Lord all the days of his life." Her prayer crossed from desire to devotion, from longing to offering. The very thing she wanted most, she placed back into the hands of the Giver.

God heard. The barren place bloomed. Hannah conceived and bore a son, naming him Samuel, "Because I have asked him of the Lord." Yet the greater miracle was not the child in her arms but the faith now living in her soul. She kept her vow, returning to the temple with her little boy as soon as he was weaned. With steady hands, she released what she had received, proving that answered prayer is not the end of obedience but the beginning of stewardship.

The story could have ended there, but God is generous with those who trust Him. He opened her womb again and gave her more children, for He will never be outdone in faithfulness. Hannah's prayer became the seed of revival in Israel. The boy she dedicated grew into a prophet who anointed kings and called a nation back to righteousness.

PRAYER THAT BIRTHS PURPOSE

Her legacy reminds every woman that prayer changes history long after the lips that spoke it fall silent. She shows us that God hears the cries whispered in kitchens and in cradles, not only those proclaimed in pulpits and courts. Her strength was not in noise but in nearness. Her victory was not in control but in communion.

Hannah's story is the story of every woman who has prayed through tears, waited through silence, and found that heaven's delay is not denial but preparation. It is the story of a wife who chose to surrender rather than strive, of a mother who saw her child as ministry, of a sister in faith who turned pain into purpose.

She teaches that prayer is not a ritual to earn favor but a relationship that restores trust. It is not the means by which we persuade God, but the space where He transforms us. Through prayer, the barren becomes fruitful, the weary becomes steadfast, and the waiting heart becomes wise.

Every mother who prays for her children, every wife who intercedes for her home, every woman who bows before her Father carries a measure of Hannah's mantle. Her voice still echoes through the centuries: Ask, surrender, and believe, for the Lord remembers.

Reflection Questions

Where has God asked me to remain steadfast when my emotions urge me to move?

What daily actions reveal my faithfulness to the covenants I have made?

How does my steadfast spirit show God's character to those who watch my life?

In what hidden ways can I mirror His constancy within my home today?

Prayer of Faithfulness

Lord of Covenant,

Teach me to stand firm when my strength feels small.

Anchor my heart in Thy promises and steady my spirit in Thy peace. Let my words be reliable, my actions sincere, and my love enduring.

As Thou art steadfast toward me, make me steadfast in all that I am called to do. May my home, my marriage, and my service reflect Thy faithfulness.

Renew my joy in obedience and my peace in perseverance.

In the name of Jesus Christ, Amen.

CHAPTER 3

Prayerfulness: Communion with God as Lifeline and Leadership

"CONTINUE *in prayer, and watch in the same with thanksgiving.*" COLOSSIANS 4 : 2

Prayer is not an accessory to womanhood; it is its lifeblood. Without prayer, the spirit starves, the mind wanders, and the heart loses direction. A praying woman does not escape her burdens; she exchanges them. When she kneels, she lays down what she cannot carry and receives what she cannot earn; peace that passes understanding.

Every woman who desires to become who God needs her to be must first learn to breathe in His presence. Prayer is the inhale of grace and the exhale of surrender. It clears the air of fear and fills the room with faith. In a world of constant noise, the woman of prayer becomes a sanctuary of quiet power. Her strength flows not from circumstance but from communion.

Through prayer, she begins to see life as God sees it. The weights that once felt crushing become invitations to depend on Him more deeply. Her words may be few, yet her faith is strong, for prayer is not performance but partnership. It is the meeting place of human weakness and divine strength. In prayer the covenant is renewed daily. Each conversation with God restores alignment between His heart and hers, keeping her household under the covering of His promise.

Prayer in Marriage

A praying wife stands as both intercessor and encourager. Her husband may fight battles she cannot see, yet her prayers reach places her presence never could. When she prays, she does not attempt to control; she covers. She asks not that God change her husband's nature but that He strengthen his calling. Her faith builds the spiritual atmosphere of her home.

Prayer reshapes her perspective. When frustration arises, she speaks first to God before speaking to man. Her tone softens because her heart has been heard. Instead of echoing the world's complaint, she joins heaven's conversation. Through prayer, she honors her husband not only with her hands but with her heart.

A wife who prays becomes her husband's quiet ally. Her words are few yet weighty. She steadies a weary spirit and lifts a discouraged heart because she has already carried his name before the throne of grace. Such prayer is grace in action. Each intercession remembers the vow made at the altar and seals again what God joined together.

Prayer in Motherhood

Prayerful mothers raise prayerful children. They teach not only by what they say, but by what they seek. When a child hears his name spoken before God, something eternal is planted within him. He learns that life has a higher order and that love has a divine source. The mother who prays for her children's souls guards them better than any fence or plan.

A mother's prayer is often quiet. Whispered between chores, offered through tears, or spoken over sleeping faces. She prays for wisdom to guide, for patience to teach, for grace to forgive. Her voice may be small, yet heaven hears it learly. God holds every tear and answers in His perfect time.

When her children wander or struggle, she does not lose hope. Her prayers form the unseen thread that keeps their hearts near to God. She trusts that the One who formed them in her womb now forms them through His will. In rayer she continues the family's promise under God, passing on a heritage of faith that distance cannot erase.

Prayer in the Sisterhood

Prayer binds women together more deeply than shared experience. When sisters in faith intercede for one another, comparison dissolves and compassion takes root. Each voice strengthens the others. A praying sisterhood becomes a fortress where the weary are renewed.

A faithful woman does not gossip what should be prayed for, nor withhold prayer from those she struggles to love. She knows unity begins at the throne of grace. When she prays with another woman, heaven witnesses agreement, and chains begin to break.

Within the sisterhood, prayer becomes a language of loyalty. Women of different ages and seasons find common ground before God. Together they remember that He listens, He leads, and He loves without ceasing. This shared intercession weaves households into one family under God.

Prayer Toward God

All prayer leads to communion with the Father. It is not eloquence or ritual, but nearness. In His presence she finds rest from striving and renewal for service. She turns ordinary duties into sacred offerings. Folding laundry becomes intercession; preparing dinner becomes thanksgiving. Her home becomes a living altar because her heart abides.

Prayer also refines leadership. True leadership is posture more than position. A heart bowed before God can stand rightly before others. Before she corrects, she prays. Before she decides, she listens. The direction of her home, her ministry, and even her tone is forged in the secret place. Her influence outruns her voice because her authority rests not in control, but in alignment with God's will. Prayerful leadership is covenantal stewardship; guiding others under the same covering that guides her.

Prayer steadies her breath and clears her sight; now the virtues that follow can take root in ordered peace.

THE WIFE AND MOTHER GOD CALLS FOR THIS HOUR
HARRIET TUBMAN

"I always told God, I'm going to hold steady on You, and You've got to see me through."
Harriet Tubman

There were nights when Harriet walked the woods with nothing but faith for a map. The darkness did not frighten her, for she had learned to listen for a Voice that spoke clearer than the wind. Prayer was her compass. When others saw confusion, she found direction. When danger drew near, she heard warning. When she did not know what to do, she stopped to pray and waited until peace pointed the way.

She had no schooling in strategy or command, yet leaders would one day follow her counsel. She carried no weapon but courage, no title but servant, yet whole families trusted her with their lives. Her authority came not from control, but from communion. She led not to claim power, but because obedience compelled her forward.

Those who traveled with her often said that when she prayed, stillness settled over them. The woods would grow quiet, and fear would fade. Her prayer was not panic; it was partnership. She believed guidance from God was as real as the ground beneath her feet. When others urged haste, she paused to listen. When they despaired, she whispered, "Hold steady," because she had already spoken with the Lord.

When freedom finally came, Harriet's rhythm of prayer did not cease. She prayed over the wounded as a nurse, over soldiers as they marched, and over the sick as they healed. She spoke to young women about trusting the Lord's voice above fear and to weary men about waiting for His timing. Her influence reached generals and statesmen, yet she never sought recognition. "It wasn't me," she said. "It was the Lord."

Her courage was quiet but unshakable. She knew when to move and when to wait. That discernment did not come from ambition, but from alignment. She followed the One who could see what she could not. People felt safe where she walked, as if God Himself kept pace beside her. Prayer gave her that confidence; it trained her heart to trust what her eyes could not yet see.

PRAYER THAT LEADS WITH COURAGE

Even after her missions ended, Harriet's home became a refuge for the poor and the elderly. She prayed over every meal she served and every life she touched. She did not consider herself finished, for prayer had taught her that God never ceases working through a willing vessel.

Her life remains a testimony that prayer is leadership in its purest form. It is not retreat; it is direction. A woman who listens before she leads carries a wisdom the world cannot counterfeit. Strength is not measured by volume, but by how closely she walks with the Voice that guides her steps.

Harriet's story belongs to every woman who faces an uncertain road. She shows that divine direction comes not through noise but through nearness. When a woman prays first and steps second, heaven still sees her through.

Reflection Questions

How does prayer shape the atmosphere of my home each day?

Do I pray for my husband and children with the same faith I use to pray for myself?

What distractions or fears keep me from a deeper rhythm of prayer, and how can I surrender them to God?

Where can I practice listening before leading this week?

Prayer of Devotion

Father,

Teach me to dwell in Thy presence with peace and purpose. Let my prayers rise like incense before Thee, and my heart remain open to Thy voice.

Strengthen me to pray when I am weary, to listen when I am anxious, and to trust when I do not understand.

May my husband, my children, and my sisters in faith feel the covering of my prayers. Let my home become a place where heaven is heard and hearts are healed.

In the name of Jesus Christ, Amen.

CHAPTER 4

Righteousness - living uprightly without fear; moral courage

"THE *righteous are bold as a lion.*" — PROVERBS 28 : 1

RIGHTEOUSNESS

Righteousness is not perfection; it is direction. It is the steady turning of the heart toward God when the world pulls the other way. It is the courage to stand upright in an age that bends. The righteous woman does not measure herself by comparison but by conviction.

Her life becomes a compass that points others toward truth, even when silence would be safer. To live righteously is to live rightly before God; when no one is watching, when applause is absent, and when obedience costs more than comfort.

Righteousness is the quiet bravery to do right, because it is right. It does not seek applause, and it is not deterred by misunderstanding. A righteous woman is not self-righteous; she is surrendered. Her courage flows from humility, and her confidence rests upon grace. She walks with the assurance that truth is stronger than appearance and that obedience will outlast opinion.

To live uprightly is to live honestly before heaven. When the heart bows low before God, it can stand tall before men. This moral courage is not arrogance; it is alignment, the strength that comes when a soul agrees with divine order. It tells the truth with gentleness, acts with honor when deceit would profit, and forgives when vengeance would feel just.

Righteousness is not loud, but it is luminous. It does not need to shout because it shines. It holds its ground quietly, anchored by a conscience kept clean before the Lord. Such integrity is not the absence of temptation but the presence of resolve. It is a posture more than a performance, a steady gaze fixed on what is good when others look away.

The righteous woman fears God more than failure and loves truth more than ease. She becomes an unmoving center in a spinning world, a stillness that others can measure themselves by. Throughout her life, heaven shows that holiness is not fragility but strength refined by faith.

Righteousness in Marriage

Marriage is the first covenant classroom of righteousness. When a wife honors her word and guards her vows, she teaches her home that truth is sacred. When she admits wrong and seeks forgiveness, humility takes root and peace returns.

Her faithfulness in small things becomes the anchor of her home. When she refuses gossip, speaks blessings, and corrects with grace, righteousness fills the air her family breathes. It grows not by rigid rule but by repeated example; each honest word, each quiet apology, each consistent boundary.

In these ordinary moments, holiness becomes habit and the home becomes holy ground. Through her constancy, she models repentance and teaches that restoration is always possible. Her steady righteousness gives her husband and children security. It tells them that goodness is not seasonal but steadfast, and it becomes the quiet inheritance they will one day carry into their own homes.

Righteousness in Motherhood

The mother's integrity becomes her children's moral compass. Before they can define righteousness, they see it lived. They learn what honesty and honor look like by watching how she speaks, disciplines, and forgives.

When she chooses prayer over panic, truth over excuse, mercy over frustration, her children see that holiness is not harshness but harmony. Her consistency weaves safety into their hearts, teaching that obedience and affection can dwell together.

Each honest word becomes a seed of trust. Each apology teaches humility. When she fails, she models confession rather than concealment. In time, her children will learn to love righteousness because they first learned to feel its peace.

Her example becomes their inheritance; her integrity, their stability. The habits of holiness she plants in her home will one day bloom in theirs.

Righteousness in Sisterhood

Among friends and fellow believers, righteousness calls a woman to consistency. She keeps her word, protects reputations, and speaks truth seasoned with grace.

When offense comes, she seeks understanding before judgment, choosing unity over gossip. Her fairness steadies others; her mercy softens correction. In her presence, trust is safe and loyalty is quiet but firm. Within the sisterhood, righteousness becomes a shared safeguard; a mutual standard that protects friendship from envy and bitterness.

Each act of honesty strengthens the circle; each refusal to speak ill preserves peace. In such fellowship, women grow stronger together. Righteousness within the sisterhood proves that courage and kindness are not opposites but allies.

Righteousness Toward God

True righteousness begins and ends in relationship. It is not earned but received through grace. The woman who abides in Christ bears His righteousness as her own, and that awareness shapes every decision.

When temptation comes, she remembers whom she represents. When accusation comes, she remembers whose she is. She walks boldly because her conscience is clean and her confidence rests not in herself but in the cross.

Fear loses its grip where righteousness dwells, for "If God be for us, who can be against us?" (Romans 8 : 31). Her courage is not self-made but Spirit-sustained; her boldness born from belief rather than pride. Her peace is not the absence of conflict but the presence of Christ within it.

Through righteousness, she becomes a mirror of divine justice and mercy; standing upright, unafraid, and unashamed. Every act of quiet obedience renews the

covenant of her faith, weaving strength into the generations that follow.

Righteousness teaches her to stand; now honesty will teach her to speak, giving voice to the virtue she has learned to live.

THE WIFE AND MOTHER GOD CALLS FOR THIS HOUR

ESTHER

"And who knoweth whether thou art come to the kingdom for such a time as this?" — Esther 4 : 14

The night before Esther entered the throne room, the palace was silent, but her heart was not. She could hear the echo of her own pulse as she prayed, "If I perish, I perish." The words were not defiance; they were devotion. Every fear, every uncertainty, every dream she had ever known was laid bare before God.

Yet as she knelt in fasting and trembling, something within her stilled. Faith began to breathe where fear had shouted. Esther had been chosen for beauty, but she was called for bravery. Beneath the crown and silk was a Hebrew heart that beat for her people and for her God. No one in the palace knew she was an exile's daughter, raised among captives, taught to honor the Lord who keeps covenant through generations. She had been silent for years, obedient and wise, but silence has a season, and hers had reached its end.

When the decree for her people's destruction spread through the empire, her uncle Mordecai's message pierced the palace walls: "Think not that thou shalt escape in the king's house. Who knoweth whether thou art come to the kingdom for such a time as this?" Those words were not an accusation; they were awakening. Esther realized that favor had been entrusted, not granted, and that divine timing had placed her exactly where courage would be required.

She washed her face, rose from prayer, and clothed herself, not merely in royal garments, but in grace. She walked the marble halls as one carrying eternity in her steps. Each echo of her sandal was a declaration that obedience is worth more than safety, and that righteousness is stronger than royal decree. She crossed the threshold where uninvited entry meant death, and the guards drew breath, expecting her fall. But the scepter lifted. Mercy met her motion. The king's eyes softened, and the tide of history shifted.

Before she ever spoke, her humility spoke for her. Her courage was not loud, yet heaven leaned in to listen. Through three days of fasting, she had learned to wait on God's timing, and now He made a way through a hardened heart. She did not rush with

COURAGE IN THE COURT OF KINGS

accusation or rage, but with patience and wisdom. She invited the king and Haman to a feast, and then another, until the moment of revelation came. In that sacred pause between fear and faith, righteousness moved unseen.

At the second feast, Esther's voice broke its silence. "If I have found favor in thy sight, O king, and if it please the king, let my life be given me at my petition, and my people at my request." The words fell like arrows of light. Truth had finally entered the court. The plot was exposed, the oppressor condemned, and a nation delivered. Her obedience had opened the gates of salvation for thousands she would never meet.

Esther's victory did not come through sword or storm, but through surrender. She risked everything to remind the world that God still reigns in hidden places. Her bravery began in prayer, was tested in patience, and was crowned in purpose. The same hands that trembled in fasting were later lifted in rejoicing, for the God who called her also carried her.

History remembers her crown, but heaven remembers her courage. She did not act for recognition but for redemption. The beauty that once adorned her became the vessel of deliverance. In her obedience, the unseen hand of God turned fear into faith and silence into song.

Every woman who faces the moment of decision, the meeting, the confession, the stand for truth, walks in Esther's footsteps. Righteousness is always tested in the courts of compromise. For her, it was a royal hall; for us, it may be a classroom, a conversation, or a culture that demands we bow. Yet the call is the same: to stand when standing costs, to speak when silence would be safer, and to trust that God's favor still extends to those who fear Him.

Esther's story is not ancient history; it is holy heritage. It whispers across centuries that courage is the language of righteousness and obedience its echo. The crown she wore was temporal, but the faith she carried was eternal. And in every woman who rises to do what is right, no matter the risk, her legacy lives on.

Reflection Questions

What does living uprightly look like in my daily choices at home and in public?

Where has fear kept me silent when God was calling me to speak?

What habits in my home either strengthen or compromise righteousness?

How can I cultivate moral courage without losing gentleness?

Prayer for Righteousness

Father of Light,

Cleanse my heart from compromise and make me bold in love. Let truth dwell richly in my words, my work, and my home.

When the world tempts me to bend, help me to stand; when fear whispers, help me to trust.

Clothe me in Thy righteousness, that I may walk uprightly and unafraid. May my courage be gentle, my integrity steadfast, and my spirit anchored in Thee.

Let my life be a quiet testimony that obedience still builds strong homes and that holiness still heals generations.

In the name of Jesus Christ, Amen.

CHAPTER 5

Honesty: Integrity in Word, Motive, and Speech

"He that walketh uprightly, and worketh righteousness, and speaketh the truth in his heart." — psalm 15 : 2

HONESTY

Honesty is the light that keeps a home from dimming. It is more than telling the truth; it is living the truth; consistency between what we profess and what we practice. A woman of integrity does not twist her words to please people or soften her convictions to avoid conflict. Her speech is seasoned with grace, yet anchored in truth. When she speaks, her words carry weight because her life has proven them trustworthy.

The culture rewards polish over purity and appearance over authenticity, yet God searches deeper; into motives, into tone, into the quiet spaces where no one else listens. He calls His daughters to speak truth inwardly first: to confront hidden pride, to confess the half-truths of convenience, and to let their hearts echo what their mouths declare. A dishonest heart can dress itself in kindness, yet leave a trail of confusion, but a truthful spirit brings peace wherever it goes.

Honesty begins where pretense ends. It starts when a woman welcomes the Holy Spirit's light into her thoughts and refuses to let deceit linger in her heart. When she yields her words to God, her voice gains authority. When she refuses to flatter or manipulate, trust becomes her fragrance. Her integrity steadies every space she touches. What she says and what she does walk in step, and through that unity the Spirit of Truth finds a willing vessel.

To live honestly is to live transparently before heaven. It means being quick to repent, slow to justify, eager to reconcile. Honesty is courage clothed in gentleness, the bravery to be real. It transforms correction into comfort and confession into communion. When truth becomes her language, her home becomes its echo, a place where promises hold and hearts find rest.

The woman who walks in honesty mirrors Christ Himself, who said, "I am the way, the truth, and the life." Her life becomes a lamp for those around her, guiding them back to trust in a world dimmed by deceit.

Honesty in Marriage

Honesty within marriage is the covenant's safeguard. It builds the trust that keeps love steadfast through seasons of joy and strain. A wife of integrity does not hide behind silence or shade her words with pride. She speaks truth in love and listens with humility.

When disagreements arise, she does not use truth as a weapon but as a window—opening the heart rather than closing it. She does not pretend peace by avoiding hard conversations; she pursues peace by speaking in grace. Her words are gentle but grounded, her tone sincere, her motives pure.

A marriage founded on honesty becomes a refuge. Secrets lose their power, forgiveness becomes possible, and affection deepens through transparency. The faithful wife does not seek to appear perfect but to remain pure in motive. Her husband may not always notice her restraint or courage, but he feels its safety.

In marriage, honesty is the daily renewal of vows unspoken: I will speak truth because I love you; I will listen because I honor God. Such integrity becomes the steady rhythm that keeps covenant alive.

Honesty in Motherhood

Integrity in motherhood is the heartbeat of trust within a home. Children may not understand doctrine, but they understand truth lived out. They watch whether our words match our actions, whether our apologies match our mistakes.

A mother of integrity keeps her word, even in small promises. When she fails, she admits it. Her children learn that humility is not weakness but strength, and confession is not shame but freedom. Each sincere "I was wrong" builds a foundation stronger than any lecture.

Honesty also shapes her tone. She does not disguise frustration as righteousness, nor disguise neglect as busyness. Her openness teaches discernment: that truth can be tender, and correction can still be kind.

The honest home is not a flawless one, it is a forgiven one. Its laughter rings truer because its grace runs deeper. Every day, she renews her quiet covenant to speak life, live truth, and love well. Such motherhood writes honesty into the hearts of generations.

Honesty in Sisterhood

Honesty within the sisterhood guards unity. A truthful friend wounds less than a flattering one, because her motive is love. When she speaks, she seeks restoration, not recognition. She keeps confidences sacred and conversations pure. Her words are a balm, not a burden; a bridge, not a wall. When tension rises, she chooses empathy before opinion. She refuses to echo gossip or harbor resentment. In her presence, women feel both safe and sharpened.

Sisterhood without honesty is shallow; sisterhood with it is sanctified. Righteous friendship grows from women who pray for one another, speak truth with gentleness, and bear one another's burdens in grace. Every word of integrity strengthens the bond. Every shared confession deepens trust. Within such a circle, women learn that truth spoken in love is not divisive, it is divine.

Honesty Toward God

Every unspoken doubt becomes a wall until it is prayed through. Honesty toward God tears those walls down. The woman who walks closely with Him hides nothing. She brings her fears, her failures, her frustrations, and her faith alike. Her prayers are plain and personal. She dares to say, "Lord, I don't understand," because she knows He already does. Such openness is not irreverence but intimacy. It is the freedom of a daughter who trusts her Father's mercy.

When she stops pretending before God, she begins to live in peace. The Spirit cannot bless what we fake, but He gladly fills what we surrender. In confession she finds communion; in transparency, transformation. Her honesty before God becomes the fountain of every other virtue; purity in motive, integrity in word, and constancy in heart.

Honesty refines her speech; gentleness will now refine her strength. For truth that heals must learn to move in grace.

THE WIFE AND MOTHER GOD CALLS FOR THIS HOUR
MARY MAGDALENE

"AND stood at his feet behind him weeping, and began to wash his feet with tears, and did WIPE them with the hairs of her head, and kissed his feet, and anointed them with the ointment." — LUKE 7:38

Mary Magdalene's story begins not in perfection but in repentance. The world remembers her for her tears, yet heaven remembers her for her truth. When she entered Simon's house that night, she carried a heart laid bare. She did not come to impress but to confess. There was no pretense left in her, only love honest enough to fall at the feet of the Savior. Simon, the Pharisee, could not see her sincerity. He saw a sinner where Christ saw a soul.

While Simon spoke in self-righteous calculation, Mary spoke only through her tears. Her silence told the truth: she knew who she was and who He was. And that honesty, humbling as it was, became the doorway to freedom.

True honesty is not loud. It does not argue or defend. It simply stands in the light, refusing to hide what is real. Mary brought her whole story to the Lord; her guilt, her gratitude, her costly alabaster box and poured it all out. Every drop was confession turned worship. When Jesus said, "Her sins, which are many, are forgiven; for she loved much," He was not merely absolving her past; He was honoring her transparency. Her love was genuine because her honesty was complete.

Later, at the tomb, that same honesty kept her waiting when others had gone. While the disciples departed in confusion, Mary remained. She wept openly; she spoke to angels without disguise of strength. Even in grief, she could not pretend. And because she dared to be honest in her sorrow, she was the first to see the risen Christ. The One who once freed her from darkness now called her by name, "Mary." The truth she had once feared now became her testimony.

There is a holiness in the tears of those who have nothing left to hide. God dwells near to the contrite because honesty makes room for His mercy. A dishonest soul cannot receive comfort; it clings too tightly to its disguise. But when we, like Mary, fall at His feet with nothing to defend, grace rushes in. Honesty opens the way for healing; it restores what pride conceals.

THE FREEDOM OF HONEST LOVE

Every home, every marriage, every friendship withers where truth is withheld. Yet when honesty fills the air, love can breathe again. A wife who speaks with sincerity, a mother who admits her weariness, a sister who confesses her struggle all invite the presence of Christ into the conversation. Mary reminds us that confession is not weakness but worship. To speak truth in humility is to anoint His feet with faith.

Her story teaches that the purest words are not rehearsed but revealed. The world celebrates image; heaven values truth. Honesty requires courage, the courage to be known and forgiven. Mary's love was remembered not because it was tidy, but because it was true. When our hearts learn to live with such honesty, our homes become sanctuaries of grace. Children trust a mother who repents before them. Husbands trust a wife whose yes means yes. Sisters trust one another when truth reigns without fear. The fragrance that once filled Simon's house lingers still wherever women choose integrity over appearance.

Honesty may begin in tears, but it always ends in worship.

Reflection Questions

Do my words and actions agree, even when no one else is watching?

Where might I be excusing "small" compromises that weaken trust in my home?

How can I speak truth with kindness, without fear of rejection?

When was the last time I asked forgiveness for breaking a promise, and what did it teach me?

Prayer for Integrity

Lord of Truth,

Let my heart and tongue speak the same language. Make me quick to confess, slow to judge, and eager to restore.

Guard my words from pride and my motives from deceit. Teach me to mean what I say and to do what I promise.

Let the pattern of honesty within me become the peace of those around me. When I fail, remind me that repentance is the road back to peace.

Clothe me in sincerity, and let my life reflect the integrity of Christ in every word and deed.

In the name of Jesus Christ, Amen.

CHAPTER 6

Wisdom — Spiritual Discernment in Decisions and Relationships

"The fear of the Lord is the beginning of wisdom: and the knowledge of the holy is understanding." — PROVERBS 9 : 10

WISDOM

Wisdom is not merely knowing what is right; it is knowing when and how to walk in it. It is truth applied with grace, conviction clothed in patience, courage tempered by humility. The wise woman does not rush ahead of God nor lag behind Him; she listens before she leads. Her discernment is not born from intellect but from intimacy; time spent at His feet, learning His voice among the noise of many. True wisdom is the art of alignment: aligning choices with His will, tone with His truth, and relationships with His righteousness.

The world calls this prudence or emotional intelligence, but Scripture calls it sanctified sight. It is the Spirit teaching us not only what to do, but when to speak, when to wait, and when to trust that silence can be holy too. Wisdom becomes the quiet rhythm of a home that seeks God's peace above every other voice. It is the lamp burning steadily on the hearth, guiding a family through the shadows of uncertainty. It steadies leadership with love, and adorns truth with tenderness.

The wise woman is not born from brilliance, but from brokenness refined by grace. She has learned that God's direction is more precious than her own understanding. Every trial becomes a teacher, every delay an invitation to listen more deeply. Her calm in crisis becomes her family's compass. She does not claim to know all things, but she knows the One who does, and that knowledge brings rest.

Wisdom is love matured. It teaches that correction and compassion are not rivals but reflections of one heart—God's heart. Through discernment, she learns when to speak, when to serve, and when to stand still so the Lord may move. In every moment, she remembers that peace is not the absence of noise, but the presence of God rightly known.

Wisdom in Marriage

Wisdom in marriage begins with reverence. It learns to pause before it answers and to pray before it reacts. The wise wife does not seek to win every argument but to win her husband's heart again and again through grace.

She corrects without contempt and counsels without control. Her words are gentle yet firm in truth. When tension rises, she remembers that the Spirit's whisper is stronger than human will. Such discernment keeps peace where pride would destroy it. Wisdom in marriage does not silence conviction but seasons it with compassion. It listens for God's leading even in disagreement and trusts that obedience to Him will never bring loss of love.

Her calm becomes a covering, her restraint a refuge. She learns to lead by leaning, to influence through intercession. Through wisdom, she transforms her home into a place where honor can dwell and where both husband and wife grow strong under God's direction.

Wisdom in Motherhood

Wisdom in motherhood is patience practiced daily. It hears what the child does not say and sees what the world overlooks. A wise mother builds not through haste but through habit, shaping hearts one prayer at a time.

She teaches more by what she withholds than by what she demands. When she chooses mercy over mockery, humility over harshness, she shows that love guided by truth becomes strength.

Wisdom teaches her when to correct and when to comfort. It gives her discernment to distinguish rebellion from immaturity, need from defiance. Her peace steadies her children's fears; her faith becomes their first lesson in trust.

She does not measure her success by her children's perfection but by her perseverance in grace. She understands that raising souls requires more listening than lecturing, more modeling than managing. In her daily rhythm of prayer and patience, her home becomes the classroom where discernment is first learned and legacy is quietly written.

Wisdom in Sisterhood

Among friends and fellow believers, wisdom guards unity. It knows that loyalty without truth is flattery, and truth without love is cruelty. The wise woman learns to balance both. She listens before she advises. When she speaks, her counsel comes from compassion, not curiosity. She prays before she corrects and encourages before she critiques.

Wisdom in sisterhood protects trust. It never uses another's weakness as conversation. It carries confidence as stewardship. Through discernment, friendships become sacred spaces where accountability feels safe and growth feels possible.

Her friendship becomes ministry; anchored in loyalty, strengthened by honesty, and softened by mercy. The wise woman's presence calms tension and cultivates hope. Her words restore dignity because they echo the heart of Christ. Such wisdom turns ordinary fellowship into holy fellowship and teaches that loyalty rooted in truth becomes the bond that cannot be broken.

Wisdom Toward God

Wisdom toward God is the highest form of loyalty. It begins in holy fear, the awe that silences self-will and awakens surrender. The wise woman does not presume to know all mysteries; she rests in the One who does. Her prayers are less about outcomes and more about obedience. She seeks direction not to justify her plans but to join His. When His answer delays, she waits; when His word convicts, she yields.

Through worship she learns discernment. The same Spirit who guides Scripture guides her steps. She discovers that peace is God's confirmation and unrest His warning. Each decision offered to Him becomes a seed of faith that bears the fruit of understanding.

Wisdom toward God deepens through dependence. The longer she walks with Him, the quicker she recognizes His tone and the slower she is to move without it. She trusts that no delay is wasted and no silence empty. Each waiting season refines her hearing until the still, small voice becomes the rhythm of her life.

In every season, she returns to the secret place, for wisdom is not a possession but a Person; Christ Himself, in whom are hidden all the treasures of knowledge. The more she beholds Him, the wiser she becomes, for His presence is the wellspring of all discernment.

Wisdom teaches her to discern, to weigh her words and guard her way. Yet discernment finds its true strength when joined with fidelity. For wisdom, once known, must be lived out through truth and loyalty.

The Wife and Mother God Calls for This Hour
HARRIET BEECHER STOWE

"I wrote what I did because, as a woman, as a mother, I was oppressed and broken-hearted with the sorrows and injustices I saw." — Harriet Beecher Stowe

Harriet Beecher Stowe never planned to shape the conscience of a nation. She simply could not look away. Born into a family of preachers and reformers, she was taught early that truth was sacred and that faith must find expression in action. Yet it was not the pulpit that became her platform, it was the pen.

She lived during a time when silence felt safer than conviction. But Harriet's heart, molded by Scripture and softened through sorrow, could not remain quiet. When she witnessed the cruelty of slavery; the tearing apart of families, the disregard for human souls, her spirit ached. It was in that ache that wisdom began to stir. She understood that truth must never be hoarded in the heart; it must be offered, even when it costs.

In 1851, as the Fugitive Slave Act tightened its grip on conscience, Harriet found herself unable to sleep. "Lord, use me," she whispered one night at her small writing desk. And God did. She began to write Uncle Tom's Cabin, not as a political treatise, but as a cry for compassion, a mother's plea that America would remember her own soul.

Each word was prayer-soaked. She wrote between household duties, in moments borrowed from motherhood and ministry. As she stirred soup for her family, her mind stirred with sentences of freedom. She wept as she wrote, pouring into her pages the grief and grace she had carried in silence. She did not write to argue but to awaken, to call a sleeping world back to righteousness.

When the book was published, its effect was immediate and electric. The stories she told pierced the heart of a nation. Ordinary readers were moved to repentance, and the indifferent could no longer claim ignorance. Her words crossed oceans, translated into dozens of languages, echoing from pulpits and parliaments alike. When she later met President Abraham Lincoln, he greeted her with a smile and said, "So you're the little woman who wrote the book that started this great war." Harriet simply bowed her head and replied, "God wrote it; I merely held the pen."

WISDOM THAT SPOKE TRUTH TO CONSCIENCE

The power of Harriet's wisdom lay not in the might of her argument but in the meekness of her obedience. She wrote from compassion, not contempt. She appealed to hearts, not headlines. Her voice was soft but steady, grounded in prayer and anchored in truth. She never confused eloquence with anointing; she knew that the Spirit alone could give words eternal weight.

Her courage was quiet, but unyielding. When critics mocked her faith or questioned her motives, she answered not with bitterness but with blessing. "If I have done even a little," she said later, "it is because God laid it upon me." That humility was her crown. The more the world demanded her applause, the deeper she sank into dependence upon God.

Harriet's life reveals that wisdom does not always roar from platforms, `it often whispers through obedience. She understood that discernment is not about knowing everything, but about knowing when to move. It is not about being fearless, but about being faithful when fear arrives. She proved that loyalty to truth is rarely glamorous, but it is always glorious in heaven's sight.

Long after her words were first printed, their echoes remain. Uncle Tom's Cabin continues to remind every generation that compassion is the truest form of courage and that conviction must always be tempered by love. Harriet's wisdom teaches that a single mother on her knees can move more mountains than armies with swords.

She was not driven by the hunger for influence, but by the hunger for righteousness. Her story calls to every woman who feels unseen in her obedience, unheard in her calling, or uncertain of her voice: God can use you mightily when you choose to listen first and speak only what He gives.

Harriet Beecher Stowe's pen became her pulpit, her prayer her protest, her motherhood her mission. Through her obedience, she showed that the truest wisdom is not loud, but luminous, lighting the path for others to see God more clearly.

Reflection Questions

Where do I most need God's discernment right now; my family, my work, or my relationships?

How can I better distinguish between my own reasoning and the Spirit's direction?

Who in my life offers godly counsel, and do I listen with humility when it comes?

What does patience look like in the current season of waiting God has placed before me?

Prayer for Wisdom

Father of Light,

Teach me to seek Thy counsel before my own understanding.

Grant me eyes that see beyond the surface and ears that discern Thy still, small voice. Make my words few and my spirit listening. When I am uncertain, anchor me in peace; when I am hasty, slow me with grace.

Fill my relationships with discernment, my home with understanding, and my heart with holy fear that leads to wisdom.

Let every decision I make bring glory to Thy name and blessing to those I love. May the peace that governs my heart become the pattern of peace within my home.

In the name of Jesus Christ, Amen.

Wisdom that Spoke Truth to Conscience and chapter 6

CHAPTER 7

Truth and Loyalty: Faithfulness to Principle and People

"WHEREFORE *putting away lying, speak every man truth with his neighbour: for we are members one of another.*" -Ephesians 4 : 25

TRUTH AND LOYALTY

Truth and loyalty are the twin threads that hold every covenant together. Without truth, loyalty becomes blind allegiance. Without loyalty, truth becomes cold and cruel. But joined together, they create the fabric of faithfulness, a life that is steady, sincere, and trustworthy before God.

Truth demands courage, and loyalty demands constancy. The woman who walks in both becomes a living witness that conviction and compassion are not enemies but allies. She is not swayed by shifting opinions or fleeting emotions; her word is her vow, and her heart is anchored in Scripture.

In every generation, truth is tested by convenience, and loyalty by pressure. The wise woman learns that integrity costs more than comfort, yet yields peace that cannot be purchased. She does not bend her convictions to gain favor or protect her comfort. She speaks truth with grace and keeps covenant even when it costs her reputation, rest, or reward.

Truth and loyalty are first learned in small things, in keeping a promise, finishing what was started, and defending what is right even when it goes unnoticed. These quiet choices become the foundation upon which trust is built. The loyal heart is not dramatic, but dependable. The truthful spirit is not loud, but luminous. Together, they reflect the steadfast character of God Himself, who is both faithful and true.

The woman who abides in truth and loyalty becomes a safe place in a shifting world. Others know that her "yes" means yes, and her silence means prayer. She keeps confidences, guards relationships, and honors commitments. Through her integrity, the people around her glimpse what it means to belong to a covenant-keeping God.

Truth and Loyalty in Marriage

Truth and loyalty are the guardrails of holy matrimony. They keep love from drifting into selfishness and commitment from fading into convenience. The loyal wife does not measure her devotion by seasons of ease but by the constancy of her care. Her fidelity is not only physical but spiritual, a promise to love in truth, to speak with honesty, and to stand with integrity when trials come.

When disagreements arise, she resists the temptation to manipulate with silence or win with words. Instead, she practices the harder path, to tell the truth in love. She corrects without contempt and forgives without fanfare. Her loyalty is not blind; it sees clearly and still chooses faithfulness.

She remembers that marriage is a covenant, not a contract, bound not by circumstance, but by sacred vow. Truth protects its purity; loyalty guards its endurance. Together they transform marriage from a fragile alliance into a fortress of trust. Through truth, she keeps her heart honest before God; through loyalty, she keeps her heart steadfast toward her husband. In both, she reflects the faithful love of Christ for His Church.

Truth and Loyalty in Motherhood

The mother's loyalty teaches her children that love does not waver when life does. She shows them that truth, even when difficult, is the gentlest form of care. When she keeps her promises, corrects with consistency, and admits when she is wrong, she paints a picture of divine integrity.

Children learn loyalty by watching it lived. They see it when their mother defends their father rather than degrades him, when she keeps her word though tired, when she honors the Lord even in hidden sacrifices. Through her example, they discover that truth is not simply taught but transmitted through trust.

A loyal mother stands as both shield and shepherd. She protects her children from deceit and guides them toward discernment. Her love is not permissive but principled; her truth not harsh but healing. When she says, "I forgive you," she means it. When she says, "I am proud of you," she roots it in character, not achievement. Her loyalty steadies their world.

Even when her children stray or misunderstand, she remains faithful in prayer. Loyalty keeps her near even when distance grows. She trusts that the God who holds them will honor her steadfast love. For in motherhood, truth trains and loyalty anchors, the twin virtues that teach children how to trust both their mother's heart and their Father's Word.

Truth and Loyalty in Sisterhood

In a culture of convenience, loyal friendship has become rare. Many build connections for applause but abandon them in adversity. The woman who walks in truth and loyalty offers something sacred, constancy.

She does not gossip what should be guarded, nor flatter what should be confronted. Her friendship is built not on approval, but on honesty seasoned with grace. She stands near when others walk away and speaks life when others speak rumors.

Truth in sisterhood means saying what is needed rather than what is easy. Loyalty means remaining even when that truth hurts. Together, they build friendships that refine rather than consume. A loyal friend becomes an anchor in stormy seas, not perfect, but present; not flawless, but faithful.

The loyal woman prays before she speaks, listens more than she advises, and honors more than she criticizes. Her friends find in her a mirror that reflects both mercy and truth. Through her steadfast companionship, the Church is strengthened, and women learn that holiness flourishes where honesty and love meet.

Truth and Loyalty Toward God

Loyalty to God begins where self-interest ends. It is choosing truth when lies seem easier, obedience when compromise feels safer, faith when the outcome is unclear. A loyal heart does not barter devotion for blessing; it remains steadfast through both drought and abundance.

Truth toward God means believing what He says, even when circumstances disagree. It is confessing sin quickly, trusting His goodness wholly, and loving His Word above the world's applause.

When others drift with the tides of culture, the loyal daughter of God stands unmoved. She does not rewrite Scripture to match her comfort; she reshapes her comfort to match Scripture. Her faith may be tested, her name misunderstood, yet she endures because her allegiance is not to public opinion but to eternal truth.

Loyalty toward God is love proven through perseverance. The woman who abides in Him learns that steadfastness is not stubbornness; it is sanctified resolve. It is the spiritual courage to remain faithful when others retreat, to keep her eyes fixed on heaven when the world's lights grow dim.

Loyalty is love that lasts; truth is love that leads. Together, they build the foundation of every home, friendship, and faith that endures. Few women have embodied this harmony as quietly and powerfully as Betsy Ross, whose hands stitched into fabric the symbol of a covenant that still waves over a nation.

The Wife and Mother God Calls for This Hour

BETSY ROSS

"I have lived to see the flag of my country wave over a free nation. May it ever wave in truth and righteousness." — BETSY ROSS

In the heart of Philadelphia, while war thundered through the colonies, a quiet seamstress worked by lamplight. Betsy Ross was not a soldier or a statesman; she was a wife, a mother, and a woman of principle. Yet in her small shop, with needle and thread, she would give shape to one of history's most enduring symbols; not merely of independence, but of loyalty to a divine idea: that truth and liberty are gifts from God and must be preserved by faithful hands.

Her story begins in simplicity. Born into a devout Quaker family, Betsy was taught that truth was sacred and honesty nonnegotiable. Her faith guided every choice, even when it cost her. When she married John Ross, an Anglican, she was expelled from her congregation for breaking custom. Yet she chose love without abandoning conviction, proving that loyalty does not mean conformity; it means conscience held steady under pressure.

When the Revolution broke out, Betsy's loyalty was again tested. Her husband joined the colonial militia and later died from injuries sustained in battle. Left a young widow, she did not collapse in despair. She worked. Her small upholstery business became a quiet meeting place for men of conviction, among them, George Washington himself.

Legend holds that when Washington, Robert Morris, and George Ross (her husband's cousin) approached her with the idea of a new flag, Betsy received them with calm confidence. They showed her a sketch featuring a six-pointed star. She listened, then took her scissors, folded a piece of cloth, and with a single snip revealed a perfect five-pointed star. "This," she said with a smile, "is stronger, simpler, and true."

It was a small act of wisdom, yet symbolic of her life, simplicity shaped by truth, practicality guided by purpose. The stars she cut were not just decoration; they were declaration. They represented a new covenant, a people united under the hand of Providence.

LOYALTY STITCHED IN TRUTH

Through every hardship, Betsy remained loyal. She endured the loss of three husbands, the burden of war, and the demands of motherhood, yet she never ceased to serve. Her home became a workshop of quiet faithfulness. When cannon fire echoed across the river, she continued her sewing, praying for the soldiers whose flag she helped to raise.

Her craft was her calling. Each stitch was an act of devotion, not to fame, but to faith. She believed that the flag was more than fabric; it was a reminder that truth must be upheld and loyalty must be lived. "It must stand for righteousness," she told her daughters, "for without righteousness, freedom will not last."

Betsy's loyalty was woven through every season of her life: to her country, her craft, her conscience, and her Creator. She taught by example that greatness is rarely loud. It is the steady work of those who keep their vows when no one is watching, who do what is right simply because it is right.

When the war finally ended and independence was secured, Betsy continued her work until her hands grew too frail to hold a needle. In her later years, she often sat by the window, gazing at the flag waving outside. "May it ever wave in truth and righteousness," she would whisper.

Her prayer still speaks to every woman who carries responsibility in the quiet places of life: that our words would be true, our loyalties pure, and our hearts faithful to the God who knits all things together. Like Betsy, we are called to stitch eternity into the ordinary; to let our faith be seen not only in what we declare, but in what we do daily, steadfastly, and unseen.

Reflection Questions

Where has truth required courage in my life, and did I answer with loyalty or fear?

How can I speak truth without losing gentleness or grace?

In what ways can I strengthen my loyalty, to my marriage, my family, my faith?

What daily practice helps me align my loyalty to God rather than to comfort or approval?

Prayer for Truth and Loyalty

Lord of Covenant,

Teach me to love truth as Thou lovest it, purely, steadfastly, and without compromise. Let my words be honest, my motives clean, and my heart loyal to Thee.

Make me faithful in promises and fearless in conviction. May my loyalty never waver with circumstance, nor my truth bend under pressure.

As Betsy stitched stars in faith, teach me to weave righteousness into my daily work. Bind my heart to Thy Word, my will to Thy wisdom, and my life to Thy glory. Let all that I am reflect the constancy of Christ, in whose name I stand and serve.

In the name of Jesus Christ, Amen.

Loyalty Stitched in Truth and Chapter 7

PART II

The Sanctified Heart

"WE PLEDGE TO LOVE ONE ANOTHER, TO BE A LIGHT TO EACH OTHER AND THE WORLD AROUND US."

-OUR FAMILY UNDER GOD COMPACT

CHAPTER 8

Purity: Clean Heart, Thought, and Intention

"BLESSED *are the pure in heart: for they shall see God."*
- Matthew 5 : 8

PURITY

Purity is not a posture of perfection; it is the practice of peace. It is the quiet work of keeping the heart clear so the voice of God can be heard. The world paints purity as naïve, as if innocence must yield to experience before wisdom can be gained. But Scripture reveals the opposite. Wisdom is born of reverence, and reverence is the child of a clean heart.

To be pure is to be undivided, one heart, one mind, one devotion. It is to live as one family under God, where no thought or affection stands apart from His light. The impure heart is cluttered with competing loves, but the pure heart is still enough for heaven to be reflected within it.

Every covenant begins here. When a woman's heart is pure, her home becomes a sanctuary of peace. When her intentions are honest, her influence becomes healing.

Purity is the invisible fragrance of holiness, the quiet scent of a life washed daily in grace. The world teaches that purity belongs only to the young or the untested, but the truth is that purity begins whenever repentance begins. It is renewed each time we turn our gaze from what distracts toward what restores.

Every mother, wife, and daughter must guard her heart from what pollutes it: resentment, vanity, comparison, and deceit. These stains are far more dangerous than any outward blemish, for they cloud the soul's reflection of God.

To be pure of heart is to choose transparency before God. It means that nothing is hidden, nothing withheld, nothing double in motive or word. The pure woman does not manipulate or perform; she abides. She keeps her spirit free of the sediment that comes from constant striving. She understands that holiness is not heavy; it is light because it is true.

When our home mirrors that inward order, it becomes a dwelling of covenant peace. We are a family under God, not perfect but preserved. Our purity as mothers and wives is not about appearance but about intention, that every meal, every word, and every act of love is offered as worship, not performance.

Purity in Marriage

In marriage, purity is not merely the absence of betrayal; it is the presence of reverence. A pure wife looks at her husband through the eyes of prayer, not measuring his flaws but guarding the honor of their union. Her words cleanse rather than corrode. She knows that intimacy begins long before the lights are dimmed; it begins in how she speaks, listens, and forgives.

Purity in marriage is the daily renewal of covenant. It is remembering that the altar we once stood before is the same altar we still serve from. The vows of the wedding day were not promises of perfection, but pledges to remain under God, patient, forgiving, and true.

When purity governs the union, peace follows. The atmosphere of the home becomes gentle. The children learn by example that holiness is not distant; it lives where love is clean. In such a home, affection becomes sacred, and faithfulness becomes freedom, reminding all who dwell there that love is safest when it is sincere.

Purity in Motherhood

A mother's purity teaches her children how to see. Her eyes become their first windows to heaven. When she delights in goodness, they learn to love what is good. When she rejects deceit, they learn to despise falsehood. When she confesses quickly and forgives freely, they learn that righteousness is reachable.

Purity does not mean her children never see her struggle; it means they see her return. Her repentance teaches them that failure is not final when grace is near. The mother who apologizes shows her children that holiness is not about flawless behavior but about humble hearts that keep coming home to God.

She lives the quiet truth that even those who wander are never abandoned. Her patience becomes a bridge for prodigals to come home. She keeps her door open to restoration, not performance.

When purity fills a mother's heart, peace fills her home. Her discipline is tempered with compassion, her instruction wrapped in prayer. Every correction becomes an invitation to begin again.

Purity in Sisterhood

Purity within sisterhood is a rare treasure. When women speak with clean hearts, unity is restored. Gossip dies. Comparison loses power. True friendship flourishes.

A pure sister delights in another woman's success as if it were her own. She covers faults instead of exposing them and prays where others criticize. She does not compete for attention but celebrates shared purpose.

When such women gather, the atmosphere changes. It feels like covenant, a small reflection of the eternal family God envisioned. In that shared light, every woman becomes freer, every burden lighter.

A sisterhood shaped by purity becomes a sanctuary of strength where grace outlasts offense and encouragement replaces envy. Through that purity of fellowship, the presence of God abides.

Purity Toward God

Purity begins and ends in the presence of God. It is the continual turning of the soul toward His face. A pure heart trusts His correction because it knows His love. It does not bargain for blessing but abides in truth.

To walk in purity is to let God search and sanctify the unseen places, the motives, the thoughts, the quiet resentments, and hidden fears. It is to invite Him into the corners of the soul until nothing remains concealed.

When we live in that posture, our love for one another becomes clear, our worship sincere, and our witness unclouded. Purity keeps that light bright. It removes the film that dulls devotion and restores vision where sin had blurred it.

The pure woman is a mirror of divine peace. Through her stillness, others see God. Her life becomes the lens through which heaven is glimpsed on earth. Purity prepares the heart for covenant; chastity protects it.

As purity orders our inner life before God, chastity orders our sacred union before one another. The next chapter calls us to honor the mystery of marriage not as restraint, but as reverence; a reflection of Christ and His bride.

THE WIFE AND MOTHER GOD CALLS FOR THIS HOUR
KATERI TEKAKWITHA

"I am not my own; I have given myself to Jesus. He must be my only love."
— Kateri Tekakwitha

Among the forests of seventeenth-century New York lived a young woman whose purity became her crown. Kateri Tekakwitha was born into a world divided, between native tradition and the newly arrived Gospel. Her heart, though scarred by loss and sickness, was unspoiled in its desire for truth.

Orphaned by smallpox, her face bore the marks of disease and her sight was dimmed, yet her spirit remained clear. She was adopted by relatives who worshiped according to the old ways, but even as a child Kateri sensed that the Creator was near and holy. When Jesuit missionaries came to her village, she listened quietly, and in their words recognized the voice she had heard in the stillness of her heart.

At nineteen she was baptized, taking the name Catherine—Kateri in her Mohawk tongue. From that moment her life became a living prayer. She refused to marry, choosing Christ as her Bridegroom. Her relatives mocked her faith; some withheld food, others beat her. Yet she answered cruelty with gentleness, saying only that she wished to follow "the way of purity."

Each day she rose before dawn to pray. She worked faithfully, weaving mats and tending crops, yet her thoughts were fixed on heaven. When persecution grew fierce, she fled through the woods to a Christian settlement near Montreal. There she was known for her tenderness toward children and her tireless compassion for the sick. Her purity was not separation from the world but sanctification within it.

Kateri's beauty was of another kind. Her eyes reflected peace; her presence quieted quarrels. She had no wealth, no title, no adornment but holiness. The villagers called her The Lily of the Mohawks, for her soul seemed to bloom in the wilderness.

She fasted often, but not from pride; her longing was to draw nearer to the One she loved.

THE LILY OF THE MOHAWKS

When she died at only twenty-four, witnesses said her scarred face became suddenly radiant, as if the light of heaven had washed away every mark of sorrow.

To this day, her life whispers what purity truly means: not perfection, but undivided devotion. In an age when innocence is mocked and desire is confused with worth, Kateri's story restores clarity. Purity is not repression; it is freedom; freedom from the chains of approval and from the noise of self. It is the quiet joy of belonging wholly to God.

A pure heart does not hide from the world; it walks through it without being stained by it. Such purity gives peace to a home and power to a prayer. When mothers keep their hearts clean before God, their children learn that holiness is not cold or distant but tender and alive.

Kateri's hidden life testifies that even the simplest tasks, spinning thread, washing garments, tending soil, can become holy when done with a pure heart. She reminds every woman that God sees what the world overlooks: the secret prayers, the silent refusals, the choices to stay true when compromise would be easier.

Her life was brief, but its fragrance endures. Purity, when guarded by love, becomes light for generations.

Reflection Questions

What has clouded the purity of my thoughts or intentions lately?

How can confession or forgiveness restore peace in my home?

What would it look like to live "undivided" before God today?

In what small ways can I teach purity to my children not by rule, but by example?

Prayer of Purity

Father,

Cleanse the hidden corners of my heart. Wash away the dust of comparison and the residue of fear. Renew in me a steadfast spirit that loves what is good and despises what is false.

Make my heart a dwelling fit for Thy Spirit and my home a sanctuary for Thy presence. Let every word I speak be honest, every thought surrendered, every motive clean.

May our family be one in purpose and one in peace, living as a promise under Thee.

In the name of Jesus Christ, Amen.

CHAPTER 9

Chastity: Sacred Intimacy and Marital Holiness

"MARRIAGE is honourable in all, and the bed undefiled: but whoremongers and adulterers God will judge." HEBREWS 13 : 4

CHASTITY

Chastity is not the silence of desire but the sanctification of it. It is the art of keeping love holy, guarding its flame so that it warms rather than consumes.

In a world that trades sacred union for fleeting pleasure, chastity restores the covenant to its rightful altar. It teaches that intimacy was never meant to be hidden in shame or paraded in pride, but cherished as a divine trust. Every covenant has a center, and for marriage that center is fidelity of body, mind, and heart.

When a husband and wife live as one under God, their unity becomes a living psalm a testimony that two can walk together when the Spirit leads. Chastity is the boundary that protects that harmony, not from love, but for love. It is the vow made visible, the quiet discipline that keeps affection holy and passion whole.

In Eden, God placed the first couple within a garden and said, It is very good. Their union reflected the order of heaven, trust without fear, affection without shame.

Sin entered when they stepped outside of God's pattern, seeking knowledge apart from obedience. Every violation of chastity since has followed that same thread: wanting the gift without the Giver. To live chastely is to return to the garden to walk again with God in the cool of the day.

It means letting our marriages and longings exist within His presence, not beyond it. When we honor the covenant bed, we honor the covenant God. When love abides within divine boundaries, it becomes light, guiding, gentle, and free. The home shaped by such holiness becomes a testimony that what God joins, He also sustains.

Chastity in Marriage

Chastity in marriage is not abstinence but awareness, the understanding that the body is holy ground. It is the daily reverence that treats affection as ministry, not manipulation.

A chaste wife does not withhold love as leverage, nor use affection as performance. She offers it as worship, a living symbol of covenant grace.

When words and actions grow harsh, chastity calls the couple back to tenderness. When fatigue tempts withdrawal, chastity whispers patience. It is fidelity not only of flesh, but of imagination to keep the mind loyal, the eyes grateful, and the heart secure.

The husband and wife who guard their unity guard their children's peace. Within such walls, trust grows tall, and love ages beautifully. Chastity is not the restraint of affection but its refinement. It purifies pleasure through purpose, teaching that to love within holiness is to taste heaven's harmony on earth.

Chastity in Motherhood

Children learn what love looks like by watching how their parents treat one another.

A chaste mother models affection with honor and privacy with wisdom. She shows that touch is tender, not transactional; that marriage is a promise kept, not a performance staged. In her faithfulness, her children learn that boundaries are blessings.

They grow secure knowing that their home is governed by love that does not wander. Each gentle embrace and patient correction becomes a quiet sermon on sacred trust. The home becomes a mirror of divine fidelity, a place where promises are kept and reconciliation is never delayed.

Such a household tells its children, without words, that holiness is beautiful and that love anchored in purity never needs disguise.

Chastity in Sisterhood

Among women, chastity often begins in conversation. It is the discipline of speech that refuses to cheapen what is sacred.

When women speak of marriage and desire with reverence, they lift one another higher. A sisterhood that guards holiness restores dignity to an entire culture.

Their unity becomes an unseen shield over their families, protecting the sacred from scorn. Together, they live the truth that our collective purity strengthens the next generation's hope.

When the daughters of God honor each other's marriages, they preserve the peace of many homes. Chastity among sisters of faith turns community into covenant where respect replaces rivalry and holiness becomes heritage.

Chastity Toward God

Chastity toward God is the fidelity of heart, mind, and desire. It is worship that keeps no corner of the soul reserved for lesser loves. Whether in marriage or in waiting, her devotion is the same, a life wholly given, not parceled by circumstance.

The woman who walks chastely before God guards her thoughts as carefully as her vows. She does not feast her eyes on what defiles or entertain what divides. Her imagination becomes a sanctuary, her attention an offering.

She understands that the truest intimacy is found not in passion but in presence, the nearness of a holy God who fills what the world leaves empty.

To the waiting woman, chastity toward God means trust; to the married woman, it means reverence. Both are held by the same hand, both guarded by the same grace. When desire is consecrated rather than denied, the heart finds peace, for the soul anchored in holiness is already home.

Chastity guards the covenant; devotion deepens it.

CHASTITY AND CHAPTER 9

The woman who keeps her affections holy now learns to offer her worship wholly. From sacred union flows sacred adoration for the heart trained to love purely is the same heart that loves God most faithfully.

THE WIFE AND MOTHER GOD CALLS FOR THIS HOUR
MARY MOTHER OF JESUS

"BEHOLD the handmaid of the Lord; be it unto me according to thy word."
— Luke 1:38

In Nazareth, the air was thick with expectation. Life was simple, measured by the rhythm of sun and Sabbath, work and worship. Mary was a young woman of quiet devotion, her days filled with prayer, preparation, and humble tasks. She was betrothed to Joseph, a man of upright spirit, and though their wedding had not yet come, her heart was already trained in obedience.

When the angel appeared, the world she knew stilled. No thunder rolled, no fire blazed, only the sound of heaven entering a humble room. "Hail, thou that art highly favoured, the Lord is with thee: blessed art thou among women." The words trembled with eternity. She did not flee or argue; she listened.

Gabriel's message shattered all reason. She, a virgin, would conceive. The Holy Ghost would overshadow her, and the Son of God would take flesh within her womb. Her first thoughts were not of fear or reputation, but of faith. She asked how such a thing could be, not as protest, but as awe, the holy wonder of a heart still pure enough to believe.

Mary's answer would alter the course of creation. She did not seek to control, to delay, or to debate. She simply answered, "Behold the handmaid of the Lord; be it unto me according to thy word." Those words are the language of chastity. They are the eternal echo of a heart completely yielded to God's purpose.

In that moment, her body became covenant. Heaven and earth met in her consent. The purity of her heart became the vessel of divine promise. She carried within her the Word made flesh not by power, but by surrender. Her purity did not silence her; it strengthened her, the kind that stands firm when misunderstood. She bore whispers, suspicion, and judgment with a peace that confounded pride. Each glance of gossip became an altar where she laid down self-defense. Her obedience sanctified suffering, and her faith built a home where holiness could grow in secret.

COVENANT OF THE BODY

When Joseph was visited in a dream and told not to fear taking Mary as his wife, he too entered the covenant she had begun. Their marriage was sanctified by trust and sealed by grace. Within their modest home, chastity became the guardian of joy.

The Christ Child grew in the safety of their holiness, love ordered, affection pure, and honor unwavering. Mary's story teaches that chastity is not about the denial of desire but its divine direction. It is the sanctification of longing, where love becomes worship and surrender becomes glory. Her life shows that what is offered to God in purity is always returned in promise.

Generations have called her blessed not for perfection but for consent for saying yes when silence would have been easier. Through her obedience, God entered the world through the heart of a woman who believed.

So may it be with us. May our own bodies, words, and marriages echo her vow: Be it unto me according to Thy word. Then our homes too will bear Christ within living covenants of love that endure for generations under God.

Reflection Questions

In what ways have I confused affection with affirmation, and how can I reorder that through prayer?

How do my words, gestures, and habits within marriage or friendship reflect holiness?

What boundaries of mind or media protect the covenant in my home?

How can I speak of love and intimacy in ways that teach my children reverence rather than fear?

Prayer of Chastity

Lord of covenant and compassion,

Teach me to honor Thee with every affection and thought. Cleanse my imagination, guard my eyes, and sanctify my body as Thy dwelling.

Let my love be faithful, my words be gentle, my touch be pure. May my marriage, or my waiting, become a living witness of Thy steadfast love.

Let our home shine as a promise kept, our hearts as altars of holy trust. Make every desire within me a doorway to devotion, and every boundary a testimony of love rightly ordered.

In the name of Jesus Christ, Amen.

Covenant of the Body and chapter 9

CHAPTER 10

Modesty; Humility in appearance and spirit

"Whose adorning let it not be that outward adorning of plaiting the hair, and of wearing of gold, or of putting on of apparel; But let it be the hidden man of the heart, in that which is not corruptible, even the ornament of a meek and quiet spirit, which is in the sight of God of great price." — *1 PETER 3:3–4*

Modesty is not a measure of fabric but of focus. It is the posture of a heart at peace, the posture of a heart at peace, content to reflect God's beauty rather than compete for attention.

It is humility made visible, a grace that reveals holiness through restraint. The world says, "Be noticed." Heaven says, "Be known." To be noticed is to seek applause; to be known is to walk in truth before God.

True modesty is not insecurity or shame; it is dignity rooted in identity. It remembers that our worth does not come from mirrors or markets but from the One who calls us beloved.

Every home under God reflects this virtue in its own way: a mother who dresses with grace, a daughter who speaks with gentleness, a family who walks in gratitude, each becomes a quiet sermon that the Spirit is present here.

Modesty does not hide beauty; it reveals holiness. The woman who walks in modesty lives in freedom. She is not ruled by comparison or pride but by peace. Her steps are ordered by reverence, her choices governed by grace. She does not perform for the world; she reflects her Creator.

Her stillness is strength. Her simplicity is sacred. She does not crave the gaze of man, for she rests in the gaze of God.

Modesty in Marriage

In marriage, modesty is a covering of peace. It guards intimacy from the gaze of the world and protects affection from the pride of life.

The modest wife understands that her beauty is a private gift, not a public show. She knows that her power lies not in persuasion but in purity, not in control but in composure. Her gentleness steadies her husband's spirit. When anger rises, she responds with calm. When pride tempts, she bows in prayer. Her restraint disarms conflict, and her presence restores order.

A modest woman does not withhold truth, but she delivers it with grace. To love modestly is to love securely. It is to rest in the knowledge that one's affection needs no audience. The wife who practices modesty in her marriage strengthens her husband's confidence and her children's peace.

She does not need to win every argument to prove her worth, nor does she fear silence as weakness. Her meekness becomes might in the Spirit. Her home becomes a place where hearts are safe and words are soft.

She is trustworthy with affection and content in quiet confidence. Her laughter is pure, her tone gentle, her joy sincere. Her husband and children feel the nearness of heaven in her restraint. Love, she teaches them, is not loud; faithfulness does not need applause.

Modesty in Motherhood

A modest mother teaches by example that true beauty begins in the heart. When her daughters watch her prepare for the day, they see care, not vanity. When her sons watch her speak with gentleness, they learn what respect looks like.

Her clothing, her words, her gestures all flow from the same source: reverence for God. She reminds her children that we are stewards of our image, not slaves to it. Every morning, as she dresses or prays, she models the truth: we belong to God first. Her modesty becomes their compass in a world that confuses exposure with empowerment.

Through her restraint, they learn the power of peace. Her me breathes calm because her spirit does.

She does not demand perfection from herself or her family, but she expects reverence. Her beauty is in her bearing, not her embellishment. She teaches that cleanliness, courtesy, and composure are not vanity; they are worship. To her, refinement is not pride; it is gratitude made visible.

A modest mother carries herself with grace because she knows her children are always watching. When she corrects, she does not shame. When she praises, she does not flatter. Her speech trains the next generation to discern truth from noise. Her silence, too, speaks reminding them that holiness often whispers.

Modesty in Sisterhood

Within the sisterhood of faith, modesty becomes charity. It considers how one's choices affect others; how we speak, how we post, how we walk into a room. A modest woman does not provoke comparison or insecurity; she carries herself in a way that lifts others rather than competes with them.

She is free because she no longer performs. Her friendships are clean. She rejoices in another's beauty, gifts, and success because she knows grace cannot be compared; it can only be shared. Her presence brings calm, not commotion.

Her words carry peace, not pressure. She creates spaces where other women exhale and remember that they are enough. When such women gather, peace gathers with them. Their laughter is wholesome, their conversation seasoned with grace, their friendship untainted by pretense.

In that harmony, the Spirit dwells richly. Together, they teach that femininity and humility are not rivals but reflections of divine design. The modest sister does not dress to outshine her friend or speak to outdo her. Her posture says, I am secure, and so you may rest too. She lives as a reminder that gentleness is contagious, and so is peace.

Modesty Toward God

Before modesty can shape a woman's conduct, it must first shape her worship. To be modest before God is to stand small in the presence of the Infinite; to remember that every breath, every blessing, and every beauty is borrowed. It is to live in continual awe that He, who could dwell anywhere, has chosen to dwell within us.

A modest heart bows easily. It does not demand but delights in obedience. It does not perform righteousness for approval but pursues holiness out of love. It does not reach for crowns but lays them down in gratitude. The modest woman prays not to be admired but to be aligned.

She longs for her life to reflect His order, her home to echo His peace, and her words to mirror His grace. She understands that all refinement begins in reverence. When she enters the presence of God, she covers her heart with humility, for she knows she stands before Majesty.

Her prayers are gentle, her gratitude sincere, her repentance swift. She learns that modesty toward God is not withdrawal; it is worship. Such modesty births strength. Because she bows to Him, she does not bend to the world.

Her peace is her adornment; her obedience, her ornament. And through her stillness, the Lord is magnified. Her humility becomes the fragrance of His presence in her home. Modesty orders the spirit; Class and Tact order our outward expression of it.

The next chapter leads us from inward humility to outward grace, from the quiet of the heart to the composure of the woman who walks through the world as a daughter of peace.

THE WIFE AND MOTHER GOD CALLS FOR THIS HOUR
BARBARA JORDAN

"IF you're going to play the game properly, you'd better know every rule." — BARBARA JORDAN

There was nothing loud about Barbara Jordan's strength. Her words carried the quiet authority of a soul ruled not by ambition, but by conscience. When she spoke, the room hushed; not because she demanded it, but because truth did.

Her presence reminded a nation that integrity is not measured by volume, but by virtue. She showed the world that a woman could rise high without losing the humility that anchors the soul.

Born in Houston in 1936, Barbara was raised in a small home where her parents taught her that discipline was a form of love. Her father was a minister, her mother a teacher, and their faith filled the house like music on a Sunday morning. There were no grand possessions, no trophies to boast of; only an unshakable belief that excellence was a way of honoring God. "If you're going to do it," her father would say, "do it right, and do it with grace."

Barbara carried that grace into every season of her life. When she entered public service, she refused to let pride or resentment drive her. She dressed simply, spoke carefully, and treated her opponents with courtesy. Her composure was her power. While others sought attention, she sought order. While the world shouted for recognition, she worked quietly for righteousness. In the heat of political life, modesty may seem misplaced, but Barbara proved it is essential.

She understood that humility does not hide truth; it reveals it more clearly. When she stood before Congress during the Watergate hearings, her voice trembled with moral gravity, not self-promotion. She spoke not to impress but to remind a wounded nation of its covenant: "My faith in the Constitution is whole, it is complete, it is total." Those words were not political; they were pastoral. She believed that justice required reverence, and that the heart of leadership was self-restraint.

Modesty, in its truest form, is not about clothing or silence alone; it is about knowing

THE STRENGTH OF DIGNITY

when to speak and when to yield. Barbara understood both. Her dignity came from the discipline of the heart: the refusal to let anger write her sentences, or vanity choose her battles. Even when the world pressed her to define herself by status or ambition, she chose instead to be defined by character. "Ethical behavior," she once said, "means being true to that which we know is right."

Barbara's life was not free from hardship. Illness would later still her steps and quiet her once-commanding voice. Yet even then, she carried herself with poise. She did not lament what she lost; she gave thanks for what remained. In her wheelchair, she continued teaching, mentoring, and calling young people to moral courage. Her modesty became a form of majesty; the beauty of a woman who understood that the truest power is the one kept under God's control.

In Barbara's life, we see that modesty is not weakness; it is wisdom clothed in grace. It does not shrink the soul, it steadies it. When we adorn ourselves with humility, we make room for the Spirit to move through us. Like Barbara, we learn to carry strength without show, purpose without pride, and conviction without cruelty. The modest woman does not compete for attention; she commands respect through the quiet excellence of her life.

So may we, like Barbara Jordan, choose dignity over display and let our composure preach peace. She showed us that the woman who bows before God can stand before kings.

Reflection Questions

Where have I confused visibility with value, and how can I return my focus to the One who truly sees me?

How do my daily choices, words, dress, presence, reveal what or whom I reverence?

What does modesty look like in my relationships, especially when pride tempts me to prove myself?

In what ways can I model to my family that true beauty begins and ends in holiness?

Prayer of Modesty

Lord of Light,

Teach me the strength of stillness and the beauty of restraint. Let my words be seasoned with grace, my presence clothed in peace.

Deliver me from vanity and the hunger for approval. Let my heart be hidden in Thee, that my life may reflect Thy glory. Where pride has taken root, plant humility.

Where fear has stirred comparison, sow contentment. Make my home a sanctuary of quiet joy and reverent order. May my conduct draw no eyes but Thine, and may my beauty be of the heart.

In the name of Jesus Christ, Amen.

The Strength of Dignity and chapter 10

_____
_____
_____
_____
_____
_____
_____
_____
_____
_____
_____
_____
_____
_____
_____
_____
_____
_____
_____
_____
_____
_____
_____
_____
_____
_____
_____
_____
_____
_____
_____
_____
_____
_____
_____
_____

CHAPTER 11

Class & Tact: Dignity in speech, posture, and presence

"LET *your speech be alway with grace, seasoned with salt, that ye may know how ye ought to answer every man.*" — COLOSSIANS 4:6

CLASS & TACT

Class is not a question of culture or cost; it is the visible peace of an ordered soul and the fruit of reverence within. It is the quiet poise of a woman who knows her worth and walks in it with gentleness. Tact is that same grace in motion, the art of truth wrapped in love.

Together they form the language of holiness made visible, the posture of peace within a restless age. A woman of class and tact does not need to demand respect; her demeanor draws it naturally. Her words heal rather than harm. Her movements reveal purpose rather than pride. Her presence brings comfort because she has learned that grace is never loud. Her light shines not through appearance but through attitude, through the way she greets, the tone she keeps, the patience she practices. Each moment becomes a reflection of the kingdom we represent.

True refinement is not born of etiquette books or social standing; it springs from holiness and humility. When a woman loves God, she naturally honors His image in others. Her voice softens because she sees value in the listener.

Her manners are not performance but worship, a way of saying, Thy will be done in even the smallest interactions. She carries herself as one entrusted with peace. She knows that every table can become an altar, every conversation an offering. She is careful not because she fears being judged, but because she longs to honor the One who sees all. Refinement, then, is not polish for its own sake but purity made visible; tact is truth that wears the fragrance of kindness.

Class in Marriage

A wife of class does not compete with her husband's voice; she complements it. She speaks with conviction, but never contempt. Her wisdom builds rather than corrects in public. Her presence steadies her home, not through control, but through composure.

When tensions arise, tact reminds her that words cannot be unsaid. She prays before speaking, listens before deciding, and when correction is needed, she chooses timing and tone that heal rather than humiliate.

She practices the gentle art of diplomacy that Scripture calls a soft answer turneth away wrath. Her calm steadies her husband's heart, her composure grants him rest. Through such grace, she teaches her children that honor and humility can live in the same house—and that both are holy.

Class in Motherhood

Children learn grace by imitation long before instruction. When a mother bends low to listen, thanks before correcting, or smiles through delay, she teaches her children how to walk in patience and peace. The tone she sets becomes the tone they carry into the world.

Class in motherhood is not about perfection, but about presence, about being fully there when little hearts are forming. She looks into their eyes, responds rather than reacts, and lets patience win over pride. Her calm becomes their compass. In her restraint, they find security.

Her dignity makes holiness visible in the rhythm of daily life, table manners, chores, apologies, and prayers. Each moment is training in tact, and every act of self-control is a gift of legacy.

The mother of class knows that the smallest courtesies become the greatest teachers. When she says "thank you" for help imperfectly given, she teaches gratitude. When she waits for a child to finish a story, she teaches respect. When she apologizes first, she teaches humility as strength. Her gentleness forms their conscience more deeply than correction ever could.

She builds a culture of peace inside her home, one where kindness is expected, forgiveness is practiced, and joy is guarded. Her presence says to her children, "You are safe to learn here." Through her consistency, they discover that class is not a costume for company but a rhythm for life.

Class in Sisterhood

Among friends, tact is the measure of loyalty. A woman of class does not share what was told in trust or speak when silence would serve better. She corrects with compassion and disagrees with dignity. She knows that tone can break fellowship faster than truth ever could.

In a world where public conversation has grown sharp and coarse, the woman of tact becomes a rare presence. She brings civility back to sacred conversation. Her example teaches others that truth and tenderness are not enemies.

When she steps into a room, she brings harmony, the fruit of a spirit governed by peace. She refuses to build connection on complaint or comparison. Instead, she honors the absent, uplifts the weary, and restores the dignity of those whom gossip has bruised. She listens longer than she speaks, knowing that real friendship grows in the soil of trust.

Her laughter is wholesome, her counsel steady, her loyalty unshakeable. To those around her, she becomes a mirror of grace, a friend who reminds them of who they are in Christ, not who the world says they should be.

A home shaped by covenant grace extends that same spirit outward: welcoming the stranger, comforting the offended, blessing without boasting. This is class, baptized in charity. Such sisterhood turns ordinary gatherings into glimpses of heaven, where women walk not in competition but in communion.

Class and Refinement Toward God

True class begins where self-consciousness ends in reverence before the Lord. Before we can carry dignity into the world, we must first bow before Majesty. Class toward

God is the refinement of worship: the way a woman composes her spirit before His holiness. When she prays, she does not rush; when she listens, she leans in with humility. Her reverence shapes her posture, her tone, and even her silence. She remembers that the God who spoke worlds into being now listens for her voice.

Her speech becomes sanctified because her heart is surrendered. A soft word carries further than a sharp wit, and grace flows from lips that have learned restraint. It is the reflection of Proverbs 31 : 26 "She openeth her mouth with wisdom; and in her tongue is the law of kindness."

Her very bearing becomes an act of worship. Shoulders lifted in confidence, eyes lifted in compassion, movements unhurried by vanity, each quiet gesture is testimony that peace reigns within. She walks through her day aware of sacred presence, not her own performance. Her composure in the ordinary becomes her altar in the unseen.

To walk with class toward God is to let every outward grace spring from inward devotion. She understands that holiness can be elegant, and elegance can be holy when both are surrendered to Him. In honoring Him, she learns that refinement is not for admiration but for alignment. Her gentleness does not yield to frailty; it carries quiet authority, for she has learned the posture of awe. Through such reverence, her very life becomes liturgy: every breath an offering, every word a hymn, every movement a prayer. Her refinement toward God orders her refinement toward man, and her peace becomes His reflection in her home.

Class and tact are the outward polish of an inward peace. They shape how we move through the world, yet they depend upon something deeper, the order that keeps both home and heart steady before God.

The next chapter turns to that foundation: Cleanliness, stewardship of environment and spirit that keeps the home a haven of peace.

THE WIFE AND MOTHER GOD CALLS FOR THIS HOUR

FROM MY HEARTH

Throughout my life, I have been known as the listener more than the talker. Words do not come easily to me, and I have never been one to fill silence simply because it feels empty. I used to think that meant I was less capable or less bold, but over time, I have come to see that listening is a language all its own. It is quieter, yes, but sometimes quiet is where wisdom hides.

I have often admired people who can speak with ease, who always seem to know the right thing to say. Yet through the years, God has shown me that while eloquence can persuade, silence can heal. There is a sacred weight to stillness when it is guided by the Spirit. He has taught me that not every moment calls for a response, and not every problem needs a solution. Sometimes, the greatest act of love is to create a safe place for another soul to breathe.

When someone comes to me upset or distressed, I try to listen without rushing to answer. I let them pour out their anger, their confusion, their heartbreak. In those moments, they rarely need advice; they need to release what has been building inside. So I let them speak, and when they have finished, I wait. I let the silence linger, not an awkward silence, but a holy one. It's in that pause that something shifts. The air softens, emotions settle, and hearts begin to open.

Then, when I finally speak, I choose my words carefully. I try not to correct or fix, but to empathize. Often, I simply acknowledge their pain or say, "I can see why that would hurt." Then I listen again. And almost every time, their next words are different, calmer, truer, closer to their own healing. It's as though that silence gives them room to hear the voice of God for themselves.

When I pray with someone after such a moment, I've learned to pray slowly. I don't rush the words. I pause long enough for the Spirit to fill what I cannot. Sometimes He gives me a verse; sometimes He gives me nothing but quiet tears. But in the stillness that follows, His presence always comes. The answer is rarely loud. It arrives like a whisper; gentle, timely, and enough to steady what was trembling.

I think that's why Proverbs 17:27 says, "He that hath knowledge spareth his words: and a man of understanding is of an excellent spirit." True tact is not about finding perfect phrasing, it is about finding peace before we speak. I have learned that if I can let the peace of Christ rule my heart before I open my mouth, my words will carry His tone instead of my own.

THE WEIGHT OF SILENCE

Over the years, this habit of listening has changed not only my conversations, but my home. It has softened arguments before they could harden. It has taught my children that patience is strength, and that a gentle answer truly does turn away wrath. There is still so much for me to learn, but I can see the quiet fruit of restraint taking root.

Even in times when I have wanted to defend myself, or when pride urged me to make a point, the Spirit has whispered, Wait. That pause has often saved me from words I would later regret. And in those moments of restraint, I have learned something about God's own nature, how slow He is to anger, how patient He is with me, how kind His corrections are when I finally stop talking long enough to listen.

Silence has become a teacher in my life. It teaches humility, because I must surrender the need to be right. It teaches faith, because I trust God to speak when I do not. And it teaches love, because I learn to put another's peace before my pride.

I still stumble. I still say too much or too little. But I have come to see that tact is not about timing alone; it is about trust. It is trusting that God's Spirit can do more through one Spirit-filled sentence than I can through a hundred anxious explanations.

So I will keep listening. I will keep pausing. I will keep letting the silence breathe, for it is often in the waiting that Heaven speaks loudest. And when I do speak, may my words be few, but full of grace, seasoned with kindness, anchored in truth, and chosen as offerings of peace. Because tact, I have learned, is more than good manners. It is ministry.

True refinement begins in the spirit, not in the posture. Class is not measured by appearance or articulation, but by the peace that governs the heart before the mouth is opened. A woman of tact does not speak to be admired, but to build; she measures her words as carefully as she measures her love. The grace she carries in silence becomes the grace she offers in speech.

Tact, then, is not performance; it is presence. It is the art of carrying Heaven's calm into human conversation. It is the quiet strength that chooses gentleness when pride demands a louder proof. Such grace does not hide truth; it delivers it with dignity, allowing conviction to rest in kindness.

Reflection Questions

When have I seen tact change the course of a conversation or conflict?

What small habits could refine my tone or posture toward those I love?

How can my presence bring calm to my household or workplace?

Where might I need to practice silence as an act of faith rather than fear?

Prayer of Class and Tact

Father of mercy and grace,

Teach me to speak with wisdom and to walk with gentleness. Let my words heal, my hands bless, and my heart remain at peace.

Grant me the discernment to know when to speak and when to be silent. Clothe me in humility that honors others and in confidence that honors Thee.

May every table I set and every tone I choose become a reflection of Thy kingdom order. Let my demeanor draw hearts toward Thee and my composure testify of Thy peace.

In the name of Jesus Christ, Amen.

CHAPTER 12

Cleanliness: order and stewardship as worship

"LET all things be done decently and in order."
— *1 CORINTHIANS 14:40*

CLEANLINESS

Cleanliness is not merely the absence of dirt; it is the presence of devotion. It is the outward expression of an inward reverence, the tangible order that springs from peace with God. When a woman tends her home with care, she is not chasing perfection she is tending a sanctuary. Every swept floor, every folded garment, every room prepared for comfort and grace becomes a small altar of obedience.

In a world that glorifies disorder and busyness, cleanliness restores rhythm. It teaches that peace is not found in possessions, but in purpose. To keep a home under God is to say, This place belongs to Him; His presence abides here. The woman of cleanliness does not idolize appearance or control; she pursues stewardship. Her home reflects her heart steady, humble, welcoming. It is not the size of the house, but the spirit within it that makes it holy.

Before the home can be set in order, the heart must be. Disarray within often reveals itself without the clutter of anxiety, the piles of unspoken fears, the hurried spirit that mistakes motion for meaning. Cleanliness begins with confession. It is a spiritual discipline: to bring the hidden corners of the heart into the light, to let God sweep away resentment, regret, and pride.

When peace rules within, order follows without. The woman whose heart rests in God finds new rhythm in her hands. She cleans, not to prove her worth, but to prepare her dwelling for love. Her home quietly witnesses as a living testimony that holiness dwells in ordinary places. That holiness dwells where every act is offered back to Him.

Cleanliness in Marriage

Cleanliness in marriage is more than tidiness; it is enderness. It is creating an atmosphere where rest is possible. When a husband returns home to warmth and order, his soul breathes easier. When words are gentle and the environment peaceful, the covenant feels tangible.

A wife who keeps her home with grace reflects the heart of the Creator, who brought order out of chaos. Her labor is not invisible; it is intercession through action. Each task whispers, You are safe here. You are seen here. You are home. And in that, the divine pattern of protection and nurture is renewed.

Cleanliness does this silently. It removes distractions, diminishes contention, and clears the way for communion. It does not demand gratitude; it creates it. Her diligence becomes a daily vow of love, a quiet promise that peace will reign within these walls.

Cleanliness in Motherhood

Children thrive in rhythm. They may not name it, but their hearts crave it, the comfort of routine, the peace of knowing what comes next. A clean home teaches more than hygiene; it teaches holiness. It shows them that God is a God of order and that love pays attention to details.

The mother who trains her children to care for their surroundings is not simply teaching chores; she is teaching stewardship. She is saying, You have been entrusted with something worthy of care.

When she invites them to clean up together, to restore what was disordered, she models repentance and renewal. In that rhythm of daily care, their hands learn worship.

Through her example, cleanliness becomes more than a household routine it becomes a language of love. When she lights a candle before dinner, she is saying, "This moment matters." When she folds a blanket neatly, she is teaching that beauty and order belong together. Her attention to detail teaches reverence without words.

Her children come to see that keeping things in order is not about control, it is about gratitude for what God has given.

Her home hums with quiet purpose, each task done as service unto the Lord. And in that peace, her children grow to understand that work can be worship and that holiness can dwell in simple things.

Cleanliness in Sisterhood

Among sisters in faith, cleanliness reflects respect. When women gather, the atmosphere they create either honors or hinders the Spirit. A tidy space, a well-prepared table, a gentle fragrance all become acts of love. Hospitality begins with preparation, and preparation is a form of holiness.

To serve with excellence is to serve with forethought. When we bring order to the spaces and moments we share, we are saying to one another, You are worth this care. That quiet diligence turns ordinary fellowship into sacred communion. In that harmony, Christ Himself is welcomed among us.

Cleanliness in service is love made visible. It does not seek recognition but restoration. When we tidy a shared space, deliver a meal with care, or arrange a gathering with thoughtfulness, we are creating room for joy to breathe. The woman of order makes it easier for others to see God in the details. Her preparation is her prayer; her presence, peace.

Cleanliness Toward God

Before order fills a room, it must bow before its Ruler. Cleanliness toward God is the stewardship of both body and spirit; a willingness to keep the temple of the soul as worthy as the home we tend.

The woman who walks in this reverence sees housework as holy work and worship as the fragrance of her day.

She rises with gratitude and rests with grace. Her prayers are simple: Lord, keep my spirit uncluttered and my dwelling filled with peace. She finds joy in small obediences, knowing that each task done with love is received in heaven as praise.

Cleanliness toward God teaches that devotion and discipline are not divided; they are two threads of the same tapestry. The same hands that scrub and sweep may also lift in prayer. Through this union of labor and love, the home becomes a hymn of gratitude, and the heart becomes His dwelling place.

Cleanliness completes the sanctified heart by bringing heaven's order into earthly living. Through purity, chastity, modesty, class, and cleanliness, the woman of God becomes a living promise; her home a sanctuary, her life a quiet testimony that the presence of God still dwells among families who honor Him.

As we turn to the next part of this journey, our focus shifts from the heart to the body and mind from the keeping of the home to the keeping of oneself; learning how wisdom, strength, and health preserve what holiness has begun.

THE WIFE AND MOTHER GOD CALLS FOR THIS HOUR
MARTHA OF BETHANY

"And she had a sister called Mary, which also sat at Jesus' feet, and heard His word. But Martha was cumbered about much serving… And Jesus answered and said unto her, Martha, Martha, thou art careful and troubled about many things: But one thing is needful: and Mary hath chosen that good part, which shall not be taken away from her." — Luke 10 : 39–42

Martha has long been remembered for her busyness, but behind that bustle was a heart that loved deeply. Her story is not one of rebuke but of refinement. She served because she cared. Her home was open, her table prepared, her every action a desire to honor her Lord.

She only needed to learn that service is sanctified when it flows from stillness.

When Jesus entered her home, Martha's hands moved quickly, kneading bread, stirring pots, arranging place settings. Every movement was meant as praise, yet her spirit grew weary under the weight of perfection. When she looked to her sister, sitting calmly at the feet of Jesus, she spoke out of fatigue rather than faith. Christ's response was gentle. He did not condemn her work; He redirected her heart. He taught her that the highest cleanliness is not only in the home, but in the heart.

In that quiet moment of correction, something shifted within her. Martha realized that love could be both active and attentive, that serving Christ required not only busy hands but a listening heart. Her kitchen became her classroom; her chores became her prayers. Each loaf of bread baked afterward was still an act of service, but now it was offered in serenity rather than strain. She learned that the fragrance of worship can rise from an ordinary meal when it is made in peace.

Later, at Lazarus's tomb, we see a new Martha, one purified through grief and grace. When Jesus said, I am the resurrection and the life, Martha was the first to confess, Yea, Lord: I believe that Thou art the Christ, the Son of God. She had learned what truly mattered.

Her heart was ordered, her faith clean, her service now peaceful rather than pressured.

THE MINISTRY OF ORDER

This transformation did not erase her strength; it refined it. She still worked, still hosted, still served—but no longer to prove her devotion. Now she worked from rest, knowing the Savior she once served in her home now dwelt within her heart. Her order no longer came from anxiety but from alignment. Every dish set upon the table became an emblem of gratitude; every act of care a remembrance of His mercy.

Martha shows every woman that God does not ask us to stop serving only to start serving from the right posture. Her ministry of order remains a model for every wife and mother who balances work, worship, and love.

When we tend our homes with prayer, our hearts with peace, and our days with gratitude, we too prepare a dwelling where Christ is welcome. And when life grows hurried again, as it always will, her story reminds us to pause and look up to remember that the Lord who calls our name twice, as He did hers, does so not to shame our service but to sanctify it.

Her story reminds us that a home is made holy not by perfection, but by His presence within it.

Reflection Questions

What areas of my home or heart feel most disordered, and what small act could bring peace there today?

How can I teach others that cleanliness is not pressure but peace?

How can I make daily stewardship cleaning, preparing, organizing an act of prayer?

What would it look like to invite Christ into the ordinary spaces of my day?

Prayer of Cleanliness

Lord of Order and Light,

Cleanse the clutter of my heart and renew the peace of my home. Let my hands work with love and my spirit rest in Thee.

Make every corner a place of comfort, every task a song of praise. Teach me to serve with stillness and to prepare with purpose.

May the beauty of order in my home reflect the peace of Thy kingdom. Keep my labor light, my heart humble, and my worship sincere.

In the name of Jesus Christ, Amen.

PART III

The Mind and Body in Stewardship

"WE *pledge to learn and instruct our children on how best to honor* GOD *with our time, our talents, and our treasures."*
-OUR FAMILY UNDER GOD COMPACT

CHAPTER 13

Education & Observation: Lifelong Learning; Discernment and Curiosity

"Give instruction to a wise man, and he will be yet wiser: teach a just man, and he will increase in learning." — PROVERBS 9 : 9

EDUCATION & OBSERVATION

True education is worship of the mind. It teaches a woman to think with humility, to see with reverence, and to observe the hand of God moving through every lesson of life.

From the first garden, learning was part of love. When God walked with Adam and Eve in the cool of the day, He invited them to notice, to name, to study, to remember. The fall did not erase the hunger to know; it only separated knowledge from holiness. Since then, humanity has chased information while forgetting revelation. But the woman who sits again at the feet of her Creator finds that every act of learning can still become worship.

The wise woman studies not to prove herself but to improve her service. She reads because truth feeds her soul. She listens because listening is love in practice. She observes because observation is prayer made visible. Her education is not confined to books and schools; it is a lifelong apprenticeship in awareness, learning to see God's fingerprints in the grain of a table, the rhythm of a child's laughter, the unfolding of history, and the quiet correction of Scripture.

The culture around her shouts, "Stay relevant, stay current, stay loud." Yet wisdom whispers, "Stay teachable." Modern learning often builds intellect while starving insight. Degrees multiply, but discernment diminishes. The woman of God refuses that divide. She seeks understanding with devotion. For her, study becomes stewardship; curiosity becomes covenant.

To educate the mind without training the spirit is to fashion a lantern without a flame. Observation is the wick that draws fuel from experience and turns knowledge into light. A mother who notices small changes in her home can prevent storms before they begin. A wife who observes with gentleness can guard peace more surely than one who argues her point. A daughter who observes the ways of righteousness gains more wisdom than a scholar who mocks it.

To learn is to love God with the mind He made. To observe is to thank Him for the world He formed. When the two meet, learning and observation, every lesson becomes holy ground.

Education In Marriage

Education within marriage is the quiet art of study: study of another soul, study of seasons, study of the covenant itself. A wise wife never stops learning from her husband.

She listens beyond words to tone, silence, and fatigue. She reads his countenance as one reads a sacred text, slowly, carefully, prayerfully. Her goal is not mastery but ministry.

She learns from mistakes instead of recording them. When conflict comes, she reviews not the failure but the lesson. She understands that love is not static; it matures like language, refined through patient translation. A teachable spirit in a wife becomes the school in which a husband grows secure. Together they practice the lifelong lesson that humility is the highest form of intelligence.

Education In Motherhood

Every mother becomes both teacher and student. She teaches her children to read, to reason, to remember, but they teach her to wonder again. Their endless questions reopen her eyes to the miracles she forgot. When she kneels beside a child discovering ants or counting stars, she joins the oldest classroom of all: creation itself.

True Christian education begins not with rules but with reverence. The mother who teaches her children to connect learning with gratitude shapes disciples, not merely students. She fills her home with words that build, books that bless, and conversations that honor curiosity. Her goal is not perfect grades, but trained vision, children who can recognize truth when the world counterfeits it.

She also observes her children individually, discerning the gifts and weaknesses of

each. One may learn through motion, another through story, another through solitude. Observation turns instruction into intercession: she prays as she teaches, asking the Spirit to form each mind according to divine purpose. In this way, education becomes a form of love, and love becomes the curriculum of the home.

Education In Sisterhood

Among women, shared learning knits hearts. When sisters in faith gather to study Scripture, they exchange more than information; they exchange light. Each insight becomes a candle passed from one soul to another.

The wise sister listens first, knowing that humility is the prerequisite for revelation. She observes the needs beneath words, the grief behind a question, the hope hidden in a testimony. In doing so, she becomes a safe place for growth.

Education in sisterhood looks like conversation seasoned with grace, correction offered with care, and celebration of one another's wisdom. The woman who learns from others never grows isolated; the woman who refuses to learn grows brittle. A community of teachable hearts is the most beautiful seminary the world can see.

Education Toward God

All true learning leads home to the heart of God. The woman of observation studies His ways as the psalmist did: "I meditate on all Thy works; I muse on the work of Thy hands." She notices providence in detours and mercy in delays. She writes mental footnotes beside answered prayers and unsolved mysteries alike.

When Scripture convicts her, she treats correction as education. When creation astounds her, she lets wonder become worship. Observation before God keeps her faith alive and childlike. Each morning she opens both Bible and window, saying, "Teach me again, Lord, through Thy Word and through Thy world." Her learning is endless because His revelation is infinite.

Education trains perception; strength applies it. Once the mind is renewed, the will must be tested. The next chapter calls the woman of God to stand firm, to turn knowledge into endurance, insight into action, and conviction into courage.

THE WIFE AND MOTHER GOD CALLS FOR THIS HOUR
MARIA MITCHELL

"Every formula which expresses a law of nature is a hymn of praise to God."- Maria Mitchell

On a quiet island off the coast of Massachusetts, a little girl named Maria Mitchell spent her evenings watching the sky. Her father, a Quaker schoolteacher, taught her that every star in heaven had been placed by God with purpose. Their telescope sat in a small dome atop their home, and night after night, father and daughter studied the constellations together. Those early lessons became the foundation of a life devoted to discovery, humility, and awe.

In a time when women were rarely encouraged to study science, Maria's curiosity could not be contained. She read every book she could find and borrowed the language of the stars the way other girls learned embroidery. While others saw only distance, she saw design. She believed that the heavens declared the glory of God and that to observe them was an act of reverence. Her learning was not a rebellion against tradition but a deeper form of worship.

She did not seek to prove her worth; she sought to understand His works. One October night in 1847, while scanning the sky from her rooftop observatory, Maria noticed a faint glimmer moving where no star had been recorded. Her father confirmed what she already suspected; she had discovered a new comet. The news spread quickly through scientific circles, and soon she became the first American woman to receive international recognition in astronomy. But when praised, she simply said, "The more we know, the more we are led to wonder." Her humility was as bright as her discovery.

Maria's success opened doors for others. She became the first woman elected to the American Academy of Arts and Sciences, yet she never saw her achievements as personal triumphs. To her, knowledge was stewardship. "We are only observers of the works of God," she often said. She believed that science and faith were not enemies but companions, each leading the heart toward truth.

THE SCHOLAR OF THE HEAVENS

When she began teaching at Vassar College, Maria carried the same telescope that once sat atop her father's roof. Her classroom became a place of wonder. She urged her students to "study, not for fame, but for use; not to elevate yourself, but to elevate mankind." She saw education as a moral responsibility—to enlarge the mind without shrinking the soul. Her lessons were about diligence and devotion, curiosity and character. In every equation and observation, she pointed her students back to the Maker of the stars.

Maria never married, yet she lived a life full of relationship with her students, her family, and her Creator. She was known for her gentleness and her resolve. When others questioned a woman's place in science, she answered with excellence. When society tried to silence her, she spoke through the language of the heavens. Her discipline became her testimony: that the pursuit of knowledge, when guided by faith, reveals not pride but purpose.

Even as she grew older and her eyesight dimmed, Maria continued to teach. She said that each generation must lift its eyes higher than the last, that every mind awakened to truth was another candle lit in the great household of God. She reminded her students that learning without gratitude becomes empty, but learning with wonder becomes worship.

Maria Mitchell's telescope still stands in her hometown of Nantucket, a silent witness to a woman who saw the world not as chaos but as choir. Her life was a harmony of curiosity and conviction, teaching that observation is a sacred calling. Through her, we remember that to study the heavens is to be reminded of heaven's Maker. She looked upward not to escape earth, but to understand her place within God's vast design.

Her story reminds every woman that learning is never a task to finish but a gift to steward. Whether she reads Scripture, studies nature, or listens deeply to those around her, she is joining the same song Maria once heard in the night sky—the song that declares, "The heavens proclaim the glory of God."

Reflection Questions

Where has God been inviting me to learn again with humility rather than pride?

What lesson might be hidden inside my current season of waiting or difficulty?

How can I cultivate a spirit of curiosity that leads my children or friends toward truth?

What would it look like to notice God's presence in the ordinary details of my day?

Prayer for Righteousness

Father of Wisdom,

Thou hast made the mind a mirror of Thy glory and the heart a home for Thy truth. Teach me to learn as an act of love and to see as an act of worship.

Deliver me from pride that pretends to know and fear that refuses to grow. Let my curiosity be holy, my study sincere, my conclusions humble.

Bless the lessons I teach and the ones I must still learn. Fill our home with words that heal, books that lift, and laughter that remembers

Thee. When I read, remind me to listen; when I observe, remind me to adore. May every new discovery draw me nearer to the Author of all wisdom.

In the name of Jesus Christ, Amen.

The Scholar of the Heavens and chapter 13

CHAPTER 14

Strength: Emotional Maturity, Perseverance, and Self-Control

"She girdeth her loins with strength, and strengtheneth her arms." — PROVERBS 31 : 17

STRENGTH

True strength is not the absence of weakness but the mastery of spirit. It is courage restrained by peace, power governed by love, and endurance anchored in obedience to God.

The world celebrates strength that conquers; God celebrates strength that endures. In every generation, women are told that strength means control, louder voices, sharper wills, hearts guarded by armor. Yet Scripture reveals a different kind of might: the quiet force of a spirit anchored in God.

A woman clothed with strength is not unfeeling; she is nshaken. Her confidence does not come from circumstance but from covenant. When fear rises, she remembers who holds her life. When storms threaten, she steadies others by standing still. Her presence becomes peace because her power is not her own.

Emotional maturity is the soul's backbone. It bends without breaking, bows without surrendering. It knows that feelings are real but not sovereign. Perseverance is strength stretched across time, faith that keeps showing up when enthusiasm has gone home. Self-control is strength refined; it protects goodness from impulse and wisdom from waste.

Every trial is a gymnasium of grace. The weights may differ, loss, fatigue, or misunderstanding, but each repetition builds spiritual muscle. Strength is not won by resistance alone; it is born of reliance. The strongest women are those who kneel often, who exchange striving for stillness, who lift their eyes before they lift their hands.

When we yield our weakness to God, He turns it into endurance. When we surrender our need to manage, He teaches us to master ourselves. This is the paradox of holy strength: it is not seized; it is received.

Strength was perfected in Christ, not upon a throne but upon a cross. He carried the weight of the world with gentleness and bore every insult without retaliation. His victory was not through domination but through devotion. The woman who learns from Him understands that real strength is not loud; it is lasting. It stands quietly at the foot of suffering and still says, "Thy will be done."

She becomes strong because she has learned to depend, not because she has ceased to feel. Her tenderness and her trust are not weaknesses; they are the very proof that His power is made perfect in her.

Strength In Marriage

Strength in marriage is measured not in dominance but in devotion. A strong wife is gentle under pressure and constant in prayer. She does not mirror her husband's frustration; she mirrors God's steadiness. When communication falters, she listens first. When burdens mount, she quietly reinforces the walls of love through patience and honor.

Her strength is not rebellion; it is reverence. She learns that leadership and submission are not opposites but harmonies within the same covenant song. Her steadiness gives her husband courage to lead; her peace gives him space to hear God. Together, they discover that strength and tenderness were never meant to compete; they complete each other.

Yet there is another kind of strength that few see: the strength of a wife who prays when she feels unseen, who stands guard in the quiet hours when her husband wrestles unseen battles. Her words become petitions, her faith becomes intercession.

When she resists bitterness and chooses forgiveness, she shields her home from despair. In doing so, she proves that the mightiest defender of a marriage is not the one who shouts the loudest but the one who kneels the longest. Through her patience, her family learns what steadfast love looks like in motion, firm, faithful, and full of grace.

Strength In Motherhood

Motherhood is the proving ground of strength. Each day tests patience, endurance, and mercy in a hundred hidden ways. The strong mother does not rely on noise or control; she relies on consistency. She learns that correction requires calm and that love often looks like persistence more than perfection.

There are mornings when her body aches and evenings when her heart does too, yet she rises again because love calls louder than fatigue. Her children learn courage by watching her begin again. When she speaks truth kindly, when she keeps promises quietly, when she prays over small disappointments, she teaches that strength is steady and gentle.

True strength in motherhood is also vulnerability before God. She admits she cannot do it all, and that confession becomes her power. When she brings her exhaustion to Him, He multiplies her capacity. She learns to trade tension for trust, fear for faith, and chaos for calm. Every act of care, every meal, lesson, and prayer is a silent testimony that God's strength is made perfect in weakness.

Strength In Sisterhood

Strong women strengthen women. In a culture that breeds comparison, the mature sister refuses competition. She uses her strength to shelter, not to shine. She stands beside her friends in truth, sometimes speaking correction, sometimes offering comfort, always guided by love.

True sisterhood becomes a forge for this kind of strength. When one woman's faith trembles, another lends her steadiness. When one falters, the other lifts. In community, strength multiplies because it is shared. The mature woman does not measure her worth against another; she measures it by how much love she can bear and still remain gentle. Together they form a shelter from the world's harshness, a circle where women learn to be strong without losing softness. Within such fellowship, comparison is replaced with compassion, and rivalry is redeemed by rejoicing in one another's victories.

Emotional maturity keeps fellowship healthy. A strong sister does not let bitterness root or gossip grow. She bears with the weaknesses of others as Christ bears with hers. Her stability becomes the soil where unity can bloom.

Strength towards God

Strength toward God is surrender in motion. It is the courage to keep obeying when answers do not come quickly, the resolve to stand still when everything inside wants to flee. The woman of God learns that reliance is not frailty but faithfulness. When she releases her need to understand, she gains endurance to withstand.

Her prayers are not demands but declarations of trust: "Thou art my refuge and my fortress." She draws strength from Scripture as from living water, finding in every promise a reason to keep going. In seasons of silence, she leans closer, listening for the still, small voice that steadies her soul.

She no longer measures strength by how much she can carry, but by how deeply she can rest in His care. Every hardship becomes an altar where she learns dependence again. Each act of obedience, no matter how small, builds unseen muscle in her spirit. Through surrender, she discovers that the greatest power a woman possesses is the grace to remain faithful when the outcome is not yet revealed.

Strength without submission becomes hardness; submission without strength becomes fragility. The next chapter turns inward to the stewardship of mind and body where health becomes the harmony of both.

The Wife and Mother God Calls for This Hour

DEBORAH

"awake, awake, Deborah: awake, utter a song!" — judges 5 : 12

Before Israel crowned kings, it was guided by judges, men and women raised by God to deliver His people in times of distress. Among them stood Deborah, a prophetess beneath the palm tree between Ramah and Bethel. Her court was not a palace but the open air; her authority was not inherited but anointed.

Israel was paralyzed by fear. For twenty years, the armies of Canaan had oppressed them with iron chariots. When men hid, Deborah listened. When warriors hesitated, she summoned them. She did not wield a sword, yet her words cut through despair like steel: "Hath not the Lord God of Israel commanded?"

Barak, the general, trembled. He told her he would not go to battle unless she went with him. Deborah did not flinch. "I will surely go with thee," she said, "but the honor shall not be thine." She knew strength was obedience, not applause. Her courage was conviction born in prayer, not pride born in anger.

When the day of battle came, rain fell and the enemy's chariots sank in the mire. The victory belonged to the Lord, yet the song belonged to Deborah. In her hymn she praised not her leadership but God's deliverance: "Lord, when Thou wentest out of Seir... the earth trembled, and the heavens dropped." She saw clearly her power had always been His presence.

Yet her story does not end on the battlefield. Deborah's strength extended beyond war; she judged the daily matters of life. Men and women came to her with disputes, grievances, and fears. She listened with patience, spoke with fairness, and reminded them to return to covenant faithfulness. Her leadership was marked not by domination but by discernment. She ruled as a mother, not a monarch, tender, firm, and steady. Through her, Israel learned that strength can be both fearless and feminine.

JUDGE OF ISRAEL

In a time when women were rarely named, God called her by name. He placed His trust in her integrity, her ear tuned to heaven, her heart set on truth. She carried the burden of a nation without complaint, for she knew the weight was never hers to bear alone. Under her palm tree, she listened for divine wisdom as eagerly as others sought her human counsel. Her strength flowed from stillness; her courage was rooted in communion.

When peace finally came, Deborah's song became the nation's anthem. It was not a cry of victory over men but of gratitude to God: "Awake, awake, Deborah: awake, utter a song!" Her voice called the tribes to remember who they were and whose they were. She did not raise monuments or armies; she raised remembrance. Her influence outlived her lifetime because it was built upon obedience, not ambition.

Deborah's legacy invites every woman to take her place beneath the palm where courage and compassion meet, where leadership is born of listening, where the mightiest battles are fought in prayer. Her story teaches that a woman of God does not have to wield weapons to change history; she needs only to stand firm in faith and sing the song God has written for her life.

Reflection Questions

Where do I rely on my own power instead of God's?

What trial in my life might be strengthening me for a greater purpose?

How can I practice self-control that reflects trust rather than fear?

Who in my life needs to rest beneath my steadiness the way Israel rested beneath Deborah's palm?

Prayer for Righteousness

Lord of Strength and Stillness,

Thou art my refuge and my might. Teach me to wield courage with compassion and conviction with humility.

When I am weary, remind me that endurance is worship. When I am afraid, steady my soul with Thy truth.

Make my heart a fortress of peace where others may find rest. Let my words build, my patience protect, and my faith prevail.

May every act of perseverance point back to Thee, for Thou alone art the source and song of my strength.

In the name of Jesus Christ, Amen.

CHAPTER 15

Good Health

"know ye not that your body is the temple of the Holy Ghost which is in you, which ye have of God, and ye are not your own?" — 1 corinthians 6 : 19

GOOD HEALTH

Health is holiness in practice honoring the body and mind as sacred trust, stewarding strength for service, and finding rest as obedience rather than indulgence.

In a world that worships wellness yet despises surrender, true health has become a forgotten virtue. We measure fitness by appearance but neglect endurance of soul. We chase results while neglecting rest. But health, in the biblical sense, is not about perfection; it is about alignment. A woman in good health lives in rhythm with her Creator body, mind, and spirit moving together in peace.

God designed the body as the dwelling place of His Spirit. Every breath is borrowed, every heartbeat a reminder that we are sustained by grace. To care for the body is to respect the Giver, not idolize the gift. The virtuous woman does not despise her flesh nor indulge it; she disciplines it for devotion. Her goal is not youth or beauty but usefulness. She strengthens herself so that she may serve with gladness.

Our generation confuses self-care with self-worship. We medicate anxiety but feed on worry; we rest our bodies while exhausting our minds. The woman of God learns a different way, the way of wholeness. She eats with gratitude, rests with faith, moves with purpose, and prays with joy. She understands that balance is not found in control but in consecration.

When she honors the temple God entrusted to her, she teaches her family that stewardship is sacred. Her children see that holiness begins with order and gratitude. Her husband sees strength wrapped in gentleness. Her home feels peace because her presence carries it. She is not ruled by emotion, appetite, or exhaustion; she is ruled by grace.

Good health begins where striving ends in the quiet confession that I am not my own. Every act of care becomes an offering, every hour of rest an act of worship, every limitation a reminder that we were made to depend on Him.

Health In Marriage

Health in marriage is the quiet work of honoring the temple God has given not only our own bodies, but the shared life they sustain. A weary body can cloud the spirit, and a restless spirit can wear down love. A wife who seeks balance in her body and peace in her mind becomes a sanctuary for her home.

The wise wife listens to her body without idolizing it. She rests when she needs renewal, not out of indulgence but obedience. She learns that fatigue can distort words and that clarity often returns with rest. When she nourishes herself rightly, she has more to give grace instead of irritation, gentleness instead of exhaustion.

True health between husband and wife is more than diet or discipline; it is communion. They learn to care for one another's well-being as carefully as their own. They share laughter, fresh air, prayer, and purpose. When one is weak, the other lifts. When one falters, the other steadies. Together they remember that love is not sustained by emotion alone but by the daily stewardship of body and soul. In caring for their health, they are really caring for their covenant.

Health In Motherhood

Motherhood demands strength of body and spirit. It requires arms that lift and hearts that listen. A mother's health is not selfish; it is sacred. When she tends to her well-being, she teaches her children to value the life God has given.

There are seasons when sleep is scarce and tasks unending, yet the wise mother learns that exhaustion does not glorify God. She understands that her children need her joy more than her hurry. She finds ways to pause to breathe, to laugh, to sit in the sunlight, to share stories instead of schedules. She teaches them that peace is health for the soul. Healthy motherhood is not about perfection, but presence. It means choosing fruitfulness over frenzy, gratitude over guilt. A healthy mother prays with her children, not just for them.

She invites them into the rhythm of rest and rejoicing, showing that care for the body is worship when offered to God. Her home becomes a place where nourishment is shared, not forced; where grace feeds the spirit as surely as food feeds the flesh. By her example, her children learn that wellness begins with worship and ends with gratitude.

Health In Sisterhood

Among women, health becomes a ministry. We were never meant to carry our burdens alone or to measure ourselves against another's reflection. When women walk together toward wholeness, they heal faster and love deeper. The healthy sister chooses encouragement over envy. She knows that comparison sickens the soul while compassion strengthens it.

A true friend speaks life into weary hearts. She listens without judgment, prays without ceasing, and celebrates the victories of others as if they were her own. Together, women create spaces of safety where honesty replaces perfectionism and rest replaces competition. They remind one another that beauty and strength come from obedience, not image.

To invest in the health of another is to practice holy stewardship. Sharing a meal, a walk, a prayer, or a listening ear becomes a sacred act. In this fellowship of care, emotional wounds find healing, and physical ones find comfort. The healthy sisterhood reflects Christ's own body, each member needed, each part working together, each life honoring the other as precious in His sight.

Health before God

Health before God begins with humility. We are not our own; we have been bought with a price. The woman who understands this truth approaches every decision about what she eats, how she rests, and what she fills her mind with as an act of reverence. Her motivation is not vanity but devotion.

She learns that true wellness flows from the inside out. When her thoughts are anxious, her body follows; when her spirit is at peace, her countenance shines. She brings her weaknesses to the Great Physician, knowing that healing is more than physical; it is restoration of order within.

Each morning, she dedicates her energy to His purpose: "Lord, strengthen me to serve with gladness today." Each night she offers her fatigue as a prayer of gratitude: "Thou hast sustained me once more." Her care for herself becomes gratitude in motion. She moves, eats, works, and rests as one who knows her body is the temple of the living God. To live well is not to live long, it is to live fully surrendered to His rhythm. Her health becomes her hallelujah, a living offering of wholeness back to the One who gave her life.

Health keeps the heart quiet and the home steady. When a woman's body and mind dwell in peace, joy naturally overflows. The next chapter invites her to rediscover that joy not as fleeting pleasure, but as the song that steadies every season.

The Wife and Mother God Calls for This Hour

FROM MY HEARTH

I have seen a great deal of trial and trauma as an adult, but over the past several years I have learned to see my trials as a gift. A gift not always recognized, rarely welcomed, and often misunderstood in the moment, but still a gift. Each hardship has become an invitation from God to pause, reflect, and grow. The refining fire may burn, but it also purifies.

There have been seasons so heavy I could not see the light of day or summon the strength to rise from bed. I have known the ache of exhaustion so deep it quieted even my prayers. On those days, I have wondered how I could lead my family when I could scarcely lift my head. How could I nurture the hearts in my home when my own felt faint?

In those moments, I have learned to step away from the endless routine and reach for something simple that awakens my soul again. Sometimes I rearrange a room, open every window, or cook something new. Other times, I take a slow drive on an unfamiliar road, or sit on the porch just to feel the sun. When I can, I walk among the trees and listen, the wind through the branches, the birds calling to one another, the steady rhythm of creation continuing whether I feel steady or not.

When change feels far away, I make small changes I can touch. Because sometimes the waiting feels too long, and I need to remind my spirit that motion still exists, that beauty still breathes all around me. And in that reaching, I begin to find Him again, the God who never left.

I look for Him in the ordinary: in the glimmer of sunlight on the kitchen counter, in the quiet hum of a song on the radio, in the scent of rain on dry soil. I try to use all my senses to notice what I had forgotten. God has gifted me this world; not a perfect one, but a living one. He has given me breath and beauty and belonging. My Savior died for me, not for a version of me that has it all together, but for the woman who still struggles to rise. That alone is reason to give thanks.

In those still moments, gratitude slowly begins to bloom. A leaf trembling in the breeze becomes a reminder that I, too, am held. A single raindrop resting on glass reflects a thousand colors when the light hits it just right, proof that even tears can carry glory.

THE RETURN OF JOY

A grain of sand beneath my feet humbles me; I am small, yet seen. And when words return, I pray. My prayers are not polished or poetic. Sometimes I weep. Sometimes I whisper. Sometimes I say nothing at all. I simply sit in His presence, waiting, hoping to feel Him near. The world says, "Give it all to God," but rarely explains how. I have learned that giving it to Him begins here: by sitting still, by letting Him see the ache, by letting Him be enough even when nothing else is fixed.

He already knows my pain. He knows my need before I can name it. But sometimes, He waits for me to know it too, to stop striving long enough to notice how deeply I need Him. And in that surrender, something shifts. The tightness in my chest begins to loosen. The fog lifts just enough for light to pass through.

Peace does not always arrive with trumpets. Sometimes it begins as a whisper, a tiny seed of joy, a faint stirring of hope. And I find myself saying, "Okay, God. You take it from here. I trust You."

And just like that, gratitude returns. Not because everything is resolved, but because I have remembered Who holds it all. His beauty surrounds me again. His presence steadies me. The same God who paints the sky each morning is painting peace across the corners of my heart. Joy has come back; not loud, not sudden, but sure. And in that quiet resurrection of the soul, I remember that God delights not in all that I do, but simply in who I am; His daughter, resting in His care.

Rest is not idleness; it is intimacy. It is the quiet confession that God can hold what our hands release. Renewal begins the moment we stop performing and start abiding, when we trade the noise of striving for the nearness of His Spirit.

True balance is not found in schedules or strength, but in surrender. It is choosing stillness not because the work is done, but because the heart has remembered Who the work is for. In that holy pause, joy returns, not as escape from life, but as evidence that His life is within us.

Reflection Questions

What habits are draining my strength instead of renewing it?

Where might God be inviting me to slow down and trust Him with my limits?

How can I make nourishment, movement, and rest acts of gratitude rather than control?

What would it look like to live each day as though my body truly belongs to God?

Prayer for Righteousness

Healer of Hearts and Keeper of Days,

Teach me to dwell in harmony with the life Thou hast given. Help me to honor this body as Thy temple and this mind as Thy garden.

Forgive me for the ways I have neglected or misused Thy gift of health. Grant me discipline without vanity and rest without guilt.

May my strength be used in service, my rest in gratitude, and my endurance in praise of Thee. When fatigue whispers defeat, remind me that Thy joy is my strength.

When fear clouds my thoughts, renew me with peace that passes understanding. Let wholeness begin where striving ends in complete dependence upon Thee.

In the name of Jesus Christ, Amen.

CHAPTER 16

Joy: Gratitude and Contentment in Every Circumstance

"REJOICE in the Lord alway: and again I say, Rejoice." — PHILIPPIANS 4 : 4

JOY

Joy is not the denial of sorrow but the discovery of God within it. It is the steady light that endures through shadow, the posture of gratitude that turns every circumstance into worship. Happiness is a visitor; joy is a resident.

Happiness depends on what happens, but joy depends on Who abides. It does not waver with emotion or circumstance because it is rooted in eternity. Joy does not ignore pain; it transforms it, lifting the eyes from what is lost to what remains.

The world chases happiness like a prize, but joy cannot be caught; it must be received. It grows in the soil of gratitude and is watered by worship. The woman who learns contentment has found a secret stronger than success. She does not measure her days by comfort or chaos but by the nearness of God.

Joy is strength wrapped in softness. It laughs in the face of despair not because life is easy but because God is faithful. When a woman chooses joy, she becomes a testimony. Her presence heals what words cannot. Her smile is not naïve; it is prophetic, declaring that light still wins.

To live in joy is to live in trust. It means believing that even what hurts will be redeemed, that even what breaks will bless. True joy is not noisy; it hums like a steady note beneath every season—the quiet confidence that God is good even here, even now.

Joy in Marriage

Joy in marriage is the daily choice to see blessings before burdens. The joyful wife does not wait for ideal days to be glad; she practices gratitude in the ordinary. She celebrates her husband's growth instead of his gaps, notices faithfulness more than flaws, and allows laughter to loosen tension.

When disagreements arise, joy steadies her voice. It keeps her tone gentle and her words gracious. Joy turns the act of forgiveness into freedom. A joyful marriage is not carefree but carefully guarded, a covenant that rejoices through weariness, choosing love again and again.

She delights in shared meals, quiet evenings, answered prayers, and small victories. Her gladness becomes a covering for her home, softening edges that fatigue or frustration might sharpen. Even in seasons of loss, she holds to joy as her compass, trusting that God still dwells in their union.

Such joy is not naïve; it is courageous. It reminds both husband and wife that holiness and happiness can dwell together when gratitude governs the heart. In choosing joy, she teaches her family that peace is not the absence of trouble but the presence of God.

Joy in Motherhood

Motherhood gives joy a thousand faces morning giggles, muddy footprints, whispered prayers at night. Yet it also tests that joy through noise, fatigue, and endless need. The joyful mother does not ignore exhaustion; she sanctifies it. She lets every small task become a hymn: folding laundry, stirring soup, reading one more story.

Her gladness is not loud but steady. She corrects with warmth, finding humor in chaos and wonder in growth. When her children see her smile through disappointment, they learn resilience. When they hear her gratitude for the day's simplest gifts, they learn worship.

Joy makes her home feel like safety. It fills the rooms as sunlight fills windows quietly, faithfully, without asking to be noticed. Even when illness or sorrow enters, she teaches that laughter and lament can coexist. She prays over scraped knees and anxious hearts, pointing them to a God who rejoices over His children.

In her, joy becomes legacy. Her children will remember not what she owned but how she rejoiced, not the perfection of her home but the peace within it.

Joy in Sisterhood

Among women, joy is a bridge. It dissolves envy, softens misunderstanding, and builds community stronger than competition ever could. A joyful sister is quick to celebrate others.

She notices God's goodness wherever it appears and names it aloud, transforming comparison into praise. She listens with warmth and speaks with kindness. Her humor heals, her words uplift. When friends face sorrow, she carries joy like oil in a lamp, steady, generous, unwavering. She believes that gladness and grief are not opposites but companions, both revealing the heart of God.

Such women become living sanctuaries. They pray together, laugh together, and refuse to let despair have the final word. In their fellowship, joy is multiplied; hope grows stronger simply because it is shared.

Joy in sisterhood is evangelism without a sermon. It tells the world that faith can still sing in the dark. It restores unity where comparison once divided and teaches that friendship itself is a form of worship when it rejoices in God's grace at work in another life.

Joy Toward God

Joy toward God is the soul's purest praise. It is gratitude expressed in motion, hands lifted, voices raised, hearts resting in trust. This joy is not manufactured; it is bestowed by the Spirit who teaches us to rejoice in the Lord, not merely for Him. When anxiety whispers, joy answers with song. When fear calls, joy calls louder. The woman who rejoices in the Lord learns that worship is warfare. She fights discouragement not with defiance but with delight.

Every hallelujah becomes a declaration that faith still reigns. Her joy does not deny pain; it defies despair. She can weep and worship in the same breath because she knows that the God who allows sorrow also promises resurrection. The deeper her dependence, the brighter her joy.

To rejoice toward God is to hand Him every outcome to thank Him before deliverance, to sing before understanding. Such worship strengthens the weary and steadies the heart. In His presence, joy is not a feeling but a force: the quiet power that keeps a woman faithful until morning breaks again.

Joy steadies where sorrow shakes. It holds the heart together when reason cannot. The next chapter calls us to consider what we treasure to guard what cannot be taken and to surrender what was never ours to keep.

The Wife and Mother God Calls for This Hour

HELEN KELLER

"Everything has its wonders, even darkness and silence, and I learn, whatever state I may be in, therein to be content." — Helen Keller

Few names capture the miracle of joy like Helen Keller.

Born in 1880, she was struck blind and deaf at nineteen months after an illness that stole nearly all her senses. The world around her became silent, dark, and unreachable. Many saw her life as a tragedy, but God saw it as a testimony.

For six long years, Helen lived trapped in frustration, her world wordless and wild. Then came a teacher sent, it seemed, by providence: Anne Sullivan. Through patience and perseverance, Anne placed language into Helen's hand, spelling words against her palm until light began to dawn in her mind. The first word Helen learned was water, and in that moment, her soul opened. Where others saw limitation, she found revelation.

From that day forward, Helen never stopped learning. She learned not through eyes or ears, but through touch, intuition, and faith. She memorized Scripture, wrote poetry, and spoke across nations of the goodness of God. Her joy was not born from what she could sense, but from what she could believe. She once wrote, "I thank God for my handicaps, for through them I have found myself, my work, and my God."

Helen Keller's life teaches that gratitude is not tied to abundance but to awareness. She learned to hear God through silence and to see Him through darkness. Every barrier became a doorway. When people pitied her, she prayed for them. When others defined her by what she lacked, she gloried in what she had received; mercy, friendship, and the grace to endure.

Her relationship with Anne Sullivan mirrored the way the Holy Spirit leads every believer: patient, instructive, gentle, unrelenting. Anne was the living parable of God's pursuit, spelling grace into the palm of a child until comprehension became communion. Together they demonstrated that love is the truest language and that education, rightly given, opens not only the mind but the soul.

LIGHT BEYOND SIGHT

Helen's story also reminds us that joy is learned. It does not appear at birth; it is cultivated through trust. Her laughter, described by those who knew her as "a melody you could feel," carried no trace of bitterness. She knew suffering, yet she refused despair. Her joy was a choice made daily, one she called "the sunny faith of the heart."

She used her life to advocate for others forgotten or unseen, declaring that every person, regardless of ability, bore the image of God. Her words reached halls of power and homes of poverty alike, teaching that gratitude can bloom in any soil.

Even after Anne's death, Helen continued her work with quiet strength. She could no longer feel her teacher's touch, yet she said she could still sense her presence; proof that love, once planted, never dies.

Helen Keller's legacy is not simply one of perseverance but of praise. She turned limitation into language, darkness into devotion, and suffering into song. Her life testifies that the joy of the Lord is not fragile; it shines brightest in those who have learned to live without light

Reflection Questions

Where have I mistaken happiness for joy?

How can I choose gratitude in a circumstance that still feels unfinished?

Who around me needs to borrow strength from my joy today?

What would it look like to rejoice before the answer comes?

Prayer for Righteousness

Lord of Joy and Giver of Peace,

Teach me to rejoice in Thee, not merely in Thy gifts. When days grow heavy, lift my countenance toward heaven.

Let gratitude become my language and praise my posture. Forgive me for the moments I have complained instead of thanked.

Fill my heart with song when silence surrounds me. Let laughter rise again where fear has lingered too long.

May my home echo with gladness that honors Thee. Turn my sorrow into strength, my waiting into worship, and let joy abide in me as Thy steadfast guest.

In the name of Jesus Christ, Amen.

CHAPTER 17

Treasures of the Heart

"*FOR where your treasure is, there will your heart be also.*" — MATTHEW 6 : 21

AMERICA BEGINS AT HOME
TREASURES OF THE HEART

True wealth is not measured by what we hold but by what we give. The woman who treasures Christ above all things learns that generosity begins in the heart long before it is seen in the hand.

The human heart is a vault of affections. What we value most becomes what we serve most. The world urges us to store up possessions, applause, and control, yet heaven calls us to store up truth, trust, and time with God. A woman who keeps her treasure in the right place will never live in poverty of soul.

The temptation of every age is to mistake what glitters for what is good. We spend our energy chasing provision instead of the Provider. We seek success more than surrender.

Yet God, in His mercy, keeps drawing us back to Himself. He teaches that the richest life is not the one with the most, but the one that gives the most. The purest treasures are eternal and cannot be lost.

A heart filled with gratitude holds more wealth than a house filled with things. The woman who treasures the Word of God will find peace even when the cupboards are bare. Her joy is not bought; it is built. She measures prosperity by presence, not possessions. She understands that what she loves most is what she will protect most, and what she protects most is what she will pass down.

Treasures of the heart are not stored in vaults but in choices. Each act of obedience, each prayer whispered in faith, each kindness done unseen becomes currency in heaven. The more we give away, the freer we become. The more we cling to Christ, the less this world can steal. A woman whose heart is anchored in eternity can lose nothing of lasting worth.

Treasures in Marriage

Marriage reveals where treasure truly lies. A woman who prizes control holds tightly; a woman who prizes covenant opens her hands. She learns that love cannot be hoarded—

it multiplies through giving. When she offers honor, patience, and trust, she invests in something that outlasts time.

Health in marriage begins with humility. The wife who treasures peace above pride listens before she speaks, forgives before she calculates blame, and guards unity as sacred. Her affection is not sentiment but stewardship; she keeps the flame of faith alive by tending it daily.

She values shared faith over status, loyalty over luxury, and companionship over comfort. Her home becomes richer not by acquisition but by affection. When she prays with her husband, laughter follows; when she thanks him for small things, joy multiplies. Her treasure is not a polished image but a living bond that reflects the covenant of Christ and His Church.

When storms come, she remembers the promise that love "beareth all things." Her strength is not in resistance but in renewal. Each act of honor and forgiveness deposits unseen riches into the foundation of her marriage, a treasury of grace that time cannot deplete.

Treasures in Motherhood

Every mother is a keeper of treasures unseen. A child's laughter, a whispered prayer, a hand held in the dark, these are deposits of love in heaven's account. The godly mother measures wealth in moments, not milestones. She values presence over perfection and knows that legacy is not what she leaves behind but who she raises up.

Her daily life is an altar of small offerings: the meals repared in gratitude, the lessons taught in patience, the nights spent praying instead of sleeping. She invests her time as currency of eternity. When she thanks God for the ordinary, she teaches her children to recognize miracles in the mundane.

When she chooses time over tasks, she declares that people are more precious than possessions. She reminds her home that hearts are shaped by attention, not abundance.

Her faithfulness plants seeds that will outlive her years: seeds of trust, tenderness, and thanksgiving.

The mother who treasures her children's souls above her own comfort shows them the generosity of God. Her joy is to give, and her reward is to see Christ formed in them. In her nurture, heaven records wealth far greater than gold.

Treasures in Sisterhood

Among women, the temptation to compare is strong, but the woman who treasures rightly becomes free to celebrate others without envy. She no longer measures worth by appearance or accomplishment but by faithfulness. She treasures testimony; the stories of what God has done in each life.

A wise sister invests her words like coin in the kingdom. She gives encouragement instead of criticism, intercession instead of opinion, patience instead of pressure. She rejoices when others are honored because she treasures unity more than recognition.

In true sisterhood, generosity replaces jealousy. When one rejoices, all rejoice; when one weeps, all kneel beside her. Friendship rooted in grace becomes a storehouse of comfort. Such women enrich one another simply by being present, by offering listening ears and open hearts.

Her richest relationships are those built on prayer and truth. They do not drain her strength they restore it. In this circle of covenant friendship, hearts become mirrors reflecting God's kindness. Here she learns that love shared is never divided but multiplied.

Treasures Before God

Before God, every treasure finds its true worth. He asks not for our things but for our trust.

The woman who treasures the Lord will never lack contentment. Her worship becomes her wealth; her gratitude becomes her inheritance. She counts faithfulness as fortune and righteousness as reward.

To treasure God is to prioritize His presence. It means seeking Him before success, listening before speaking, and serving before storing. When she begins each day with prayer, her schedule becomes sanctified; when she ends it with thanksgiving, her rest becomes holy.

She does not fear loss, for her joy is in what cannot perish. She finds abundance in simplicity and strength in surrender. Her generosity flows from a heart convinced that she owns nothing but is entrusted with everything.

Time itself becomes her most sacred offering. She learns that each sunrise is a fresh deposit of grace, a trust from the One who numbers her days. "So teach us to number our days, that we may apply our hearts unto wisdom." — Psalm 90 : 12. When she spends her time in love and obedience, she converts it into treasure eternal.

When a woman learns to treasure what is eternal, her hands begin to serve what is lasting. The love that once filled her heart now overflows into her home, her marriage, her community. What she guards within, she begins to give without. In the next part, we turn from the inward keeping of virtue to the outward ministry of daily life, where the treasures of the heart become the labors of love that shape a household under God.

The Wife and Mother God Calls for This Hour

MARY OF BETHANY

"she hath done what she could." — mark 14 : 8

Mary of Bethany is remembered not for what she kept but for what she gave away. She lived in a small village near Jerusalem with her sister Martha and her brother Lazarus. Jesus often visited their home, finding rest in their friendship. Martha served, but Mary sat at His feet. In her stillness, she found revelation; in her listening, she discovered the treasure that could not be taken from her.

While others hurried to prepare the meal, Mary lingered in His presence. Every word He spoke became another jewel for her soul. She learned that devotion is not measured in motion but in attention. She gave Him her ears before she ever gave Him her offering. Her treasure was formed in quiet places long before it was poured out in public.

When Lazarus died, Mary fell at the Lord's feet in grief yet faith, saying, "Lord, if Thou hadst been here, my brother had not died." Her love was honest, her trust unbroken. She did not hide her sorrow; she carried it to the One who could redeem it. Jesus met her tears with power and called her brother from the tomb. From that moment her heart overflowed with gratitude that could not be contained. Every breath of Lazarus was a reminder that nothing offered to Christ is ever truly lost.

As the days passed and the shadow of the cross grew near, Mary sensed something few others did. She had heard His words about suffering and resurrection, and though she could not understand them fully, her spirit was stirred to honor Him while there was still time. She prepared her offering with quiet determination, choosing the purest oil, sealed in alabaster, meant for burial. For her, this act was not duty but destiny, a love offering before the world would comprehend its meaning.

When the evening came, and the house of Simon filled with voices and laughter, Mary entered the room carrying her jar. The men reclined at the table, their conversation heavy with questions about the future. Without a word, she knelt beside Jesus and broke the vessel. The fragrance burst into the air, sweet and strong, filling every corner of the room. It was the scent of surrender.

THE ALABASTER OFFERING

She poured the oil upon His feet and wiped them with her hair. No one instructed her to do this. Love compelled her. Her worship needed no words. It was gratitude made visible, faith made fragrant. The cost did not matter, for she had already counted Him worth everything.

The disciples murmured among themselves that her gift was wasteful, that such wealth could have been sold and given to the poor. They saw only the price; she saw the Person. Jesus silenced their criticism with tenderness: "Let her alone. She hath done a good work upon me." He saw what they could not her devotion anointing Him for burial, her faith preparing His body for glory.

Mary's act was prophetic. She offered her treasure before anyone else understood the hour. Her gift was not performance but participation in the story of redemption. In that moment, heaven recorded her act, and Jesus promised it would be remembered wherever the gospel was preached. Two millennia later, the fragrance of her worship still lingers.

Her treasure was her trust. Her strength was her stillness. She reminds every believer that devotion requires surrender and that love, to be real, must cost something. Mary teaches that what is poured out for Christ is never wasted, for the heart that treasures Him above all else cannot be impoverished. The perfume fades, but the obedience endures.

For the woman who chooses Christ above comfort, generosity becomes joy. She learns to release rather than retain, to worship rather than worry, to give before she grasps. Mary's story is a mirror of eternal truth: that what is given to God remains forever.

Reflection Questions

What am I protecting that God has asked me to release?

Where have I confused possession with peace?

How can I give more freely from a place of gratitude rather than guilt?

What would it look like for my love to cost me something today?

Prayer for Righteousness

Lord of Heaven and Keeper of Hearts,

Teach me to treasure what matters most. Wean my desires from the fleeting and fix my gaze upon the eternal.

Forgive me for holding tightly to what was meant to be given away. Fill me with gratitude that gives freely, love that listens, and peace that endures.

Let my life carry the fragrance of devotion that pleases Thee. May every act of generosity be worship in disguise.

When my heart grows anxious, remind me that Thou art my portion and my prize. Let my treasures rest safely in Thy keeping forever.

In the name of Jesus Christ, Amen

The Alabaster Offering and chapter 17

CHAPTER 18

Guarding Against Other Gods

"LITTLE *children, keep yourselves from idols. Amen."* — 1 JOHN 5:21

America Begins At Home

GUARDING AGAINST OTHER GODS

To guard against other gods is to keep the heart pure when the world demands divided worship. Idolatry no longer arrives with carved stone and golden image. It comes in the glow of screens, the applause of followers, and the pursuit of comfort over calling. Modern idols smile. They promise ease, belonging, beauty, and control, yet they steal affection that belongs only to God.

To guard against other gods is not to reject the good things of creation but to return them to their proper order. The heart becomes holy when gratitude replaces grasping. Every gift misused becomes a god; every gift received with thanksgiving becomes worship.

The old idols of Baal and Mammon have simply learned new names: success, influence, entertainment, independence, and self. They promise empowerment while demanding exhaustion. They tell us to build our worth through constant visibility, to shape our identity through image rather than integrity.

The woman of God must learn to recognize these false sanctuaries for what they are: altars that require her peace as sacrifice. A heart under God is a guarded heart. It does not fear the world, yet it refuses to be formed by it. Guarding against other gods is not paranoia but protection.

It is the mother watching over her children's hearts as carefully as she watches over their steps. It is the wife refusing to let comparison poison affection. It is the daughter of God closing her eyes to noise so she can hear His voice again.

The true worshipper does not divide her devotion. She learns to hold every affection beneath heaven's authority, knowing that what she refuses to idolize, God will purify and multiply. Her freedom begins when she can say: "Thou alone, O Lord, art worthy."

Guarding In Marriage

Idolatry often creeps quietly into marriage through expectation. A husband becomes an idol when we demand from him what only God can provide: identity, affirmation, or unbroken peace. Love loses its joy when it becomes worship.

The wise wife releases her spouse from being savior and restores him to being partner. She learns to pray rather than control, to bless rather than burden. When affection is placed under God's rule, love deepens rather than drains.

True marital devotion bows together before one throne. Each spouse strengthens the other by seeking holiness more than happiness. When both kneel to the same Lord, their covenant becomes secure, not because they are flawless, but because they are forgiven.

Guarding In Motherhood

The mother's heart is easily tempted by the idol of outcome. She measures her worth by her children's success, behavior, or approval. Yet children were never meant to be mirrors of perfection; they are souls entrusted for formation.

A mother guards against idols when she releases the illusion of control and remembers that God loves her children more than she ever could.

Her stewardship is holy because it is humble. She prays rather than performs. She listens to God for their sake and lets His Word, not comparison, define what faithfulness looks like in her home. When she entrusts the future to Him, her children grow not under pressure, but under peace.

Guarding In Sisterhood

Within the fellowship of women, idols often hide beneath admiration. Comparison becomes quiet idolatry when we measure one another instead of magnifying God together. Guarding against other gods in sisterhood means celebrating another's blessing without feeling diminished.

The faithful sister rejoices when another is honored because she knows every gift is for the good of the whole body. She prays that no jealousy take root, no bitterness divide. In her speech there is no envy, only edification. The bonds of faith remain unbroken because her worship is undivided.

When women guard one another's dignity instead of competing for it, they mirror heaven's unity. The home, the church, and the culture are healed when women lay down rivalry and lift up reverence.

Guarding Toward God

Every idol begins in the imagination before it reaches the hands. To guard against other gods, the believer must return daily to the altar of surrender. She asks: "What has my heart begun to love more than obedience?"

True worship flows from remembrance. Gratitude breaks the spell of idolatry because it reorders desire. A thankful heart cannot serve two masters; it bows gladly to one. When God is honored first, all else finds right proportion.

Guarding the heart is therefore a daily practice of awareness and repentance. The woman of God inspects her motives the way a gardener inspects roots. She knows that neglect invites overgrowth, but attention brings fruit. Her vigilance is peace, not fear. She is not afraid of the world's noise because she has chosen the stillness of His presence.

Guarding against other gods purifies our devotion. Once the heart is freed from false worship, it is ready to serve through nurture, the holy work of shaping lives under God's care.

The Wife and Mother God Calls for This Hour

RAHAB

"the Lord your God, He is God in heaven above, and in earth beneath." — JOSHUA 2 : 11

The city of Jericho pulsed with worship, but not of heaven. Its altars smoked before Baal, its festivals honored Astarte, the goddess of fertility, and its towers bore carved symbols of power that could not save. Within those walls lived Rahab; a woman of reputation, known for her past yet remembered by heaven for her faith.

In a land that traded purity for pleasure and sacrifice for gain, Rahab's heart began to stir with quiet conviction. She had heard the stories: the Red Sea dividing, Pharaoh's armies swallowed by the waves, the manna that fell like morning dew. Her city trembled at these tales, but Rahab listened differently. Where others feared, she discerned truth. She sensed that these wonders were not mere conquest, they were covenant.

The gods of Jericho demanded constant appeasement and offered no peace. Rahab had seen their worship up close: ritual without mercy, passion without purity, religion without rest. But in the God of Israel, she recognized something new; a holiness that was both powerful and good. So when two Israelite spies sought refuge within her house, she made a choice that would change eternity. She hid them beneath stalks of flax on her roof, and with trembling honesty confessed her faith: "The Lord your God, He is God in heaven above, and in earth beneath."

That single declaration shattered generations of idolatry. In a city devoted to false gods, one woman dared to believe in the true One. Her faith was not born of sight but of surrender. She risked her life for a God she had only heard of, trusting that His mercy as greater than her past.

Rahab's home stood in the outer wall, a fitting symbol of her life on the edge between two worlds. As the armies of Israel surrounded the city, she marked her window with a scarlet cord, a sign of her covenant and her trust. That crimson thread told the story of every heart that ever turned from idols: rescued not by worthiness but by grace.

TURNING FROM FALSE GODS TO THE LIVING GOD

When Jericho fell, Rahab's household alone was spared. She left behind the smoke of false worship and stepped into the camp of God's people. There she began anew, no longer the woman of Jericho but a daughter of Israel. Her name joined the lineage of redemption; through her came Boaz, through Boaz came David, and through David came Christ. From idolatry rose inheritance.

Rahab's story reminds us that guarding against other gods begins not with rules, but with revelation. The human heart will always worship something; the question is whom. False gods still whisper today: success, self-image, comfort, control. They promise freedom but enslave the soul. Yet the same grace that reached Rahab reaches us. The God who entered her story enters ours, inviting us to exchange idols for intimacy.

Every woman who keeps her heart for the Lord becomes a defender of truth in her home. She teaches her children that no screen or status can satisfy the soul. She remembers that worship belongs not only in song but in how we spend our attention, affection, and time. Her home becomes a fortress of devotion where the presence of God is prized above every possession.

Rahab's window overlooked ruin, yet framed redemption. Her faith turned destruction into deliverance. In her, we learn that guarding against other gods is not about living in fear of losing holiness; it is about living in awe of the One who restores it.

When false gods fall silent, the true God speaks peace.`

Reflection Questions

What do I most fear losing, and what does that reveal about where my trust lies?

How have good gifts, family, work, ministry, or success, quietly taken the place of the Giver in my thoughts?

What daily practices could help me keep gratitude greater than grasping?

How can I guard my children's hearts from the idols I have already learned to resist?

Prayer for Righteousness

Lord of all creation,

Cleanse my heart from every affection that competes with Thee. Teach me to see Thy hand in every good gift and to hold each one with open palms.

Break the idols that promise peace but steal my worship. Let my love be ordered, my desires purified, and my thoughts anchored in truth.

Where I have exalted self, restore surrender. Where I have sought control, restore contentment. May my household remember that all blessings belong to Thee. Keep our hearts united, undivided, and faithful until the end.

In the name of Jesus Christ, Amen.

PART IV

The Ministry of Home and Family

"WE *pledge to strengthen our faith and families ties, to uplift and encourage and uplift one another, and to stand firm in the face of any effort within or without to dim our light, love, or liberty to one another."*
-OUR FAMILY UNDER GOD COMPACT

CHAPTER 19

Nurture: Teaching, Tending, and Shaping Hearts

"SHE *openeth her mouth with wisdom; and in her tongue is the law of kindness.*"

— PROVERBS 31:26

NURTURE

Nurture is love made patient, truth spoken softly and lived daily. To nurture is to partner with God in the shaping of souls. It is the sacred work of cultivation, where love becomes instruction and tenderness becomes strength. A nurturing woman is not merely gentle; she is wise enough to see potential and faithful enough to stay until it blooms.

Our culture prizes production more than presence. It measures value by achievement and efficiency rather than care. Yet heaven's order begins with nurture. The first command given to humanity, "Be fruitful and multiply" was not a charge of conquest, but of cultivation. God entrusts women with a reflection of His own heart: to bring forth, to protect, and to teach what is good.

Nurture is not confined to motherhood. It is the spirit of discipleship that flows through every relationship. The woman who nurtures her marriage strengthens the foundation of home. The woman who nurtures her friendships heals division. The woman who nurtures her faith sustains generations.

The counterfeit of nurture is neglect; whether through distraction, resentment, or weariness. The nurturing woman learns to guard her tenderness from the world's hardness. She does not allow exhaustion to make her indifferent or hurry to make her harsh. Her care is not sentimental but spiritual; it flows from communion with God.

Every act of nurture is a seed of peace. Each word of encouragement, each quiet correction, each gentle boundary builds a garden where others may rest and grow. The Lord Himself walks through such gardens. "I will walk among you, and will be your God, and ye shall be my people." The home that welcomes His presence becomes a living sanctuary where love is the language and patience the atmosphere.

Nurture in Marriage

In marriage, nurture takes the shape of steady encouragement. It is not flattery or indulgence, but the art of seeing through weakness to potential. A nurturing wife builds her husband with words that restore rather than erode. She prays when pride would scold, and she listens when frustration would speak first.

The world tells women to demand leadership through control, yet Scripture teaches influence through grace. The heart of a husband flourishes under kindness. The nurturing wife does not compete for authority; she cultivates unity. Her presence becomes rest to her husband because she tends to the soil of peace between them.

When disappointment or misunderstanding arises, she returns to prayer before persuasion. She asks not how to win an argument but how to win a heart. In nurturing love, she teaches trust, and in trusting God, she teaches love.

Nurture in Motherhood

In motherhood, nurture is the patient rhythm of teaching, correcting, comforting, and releasing. A mother's voice is the first language her children associate with love. Every word spoken in faith plants the knowledge of God deeper than any lesson can reach.

A nurturing mother is both gentle and firm. She gives freedom within the frame of obedience. She trains her children not only to behave, but to believe. Her tenderness does not excuse sin but restores the sinner. When she disciplines with calm authority, her children learn that correction is not rejection but protection.

In moments of fatigue or frustration, she remembers that nurture is eternal work disguised as ordinary days. Meals prepared, clothes folded, tears wiped; all become offerings when done with prayerful heart. Through her presence, children learn that God is near.

The enemy seeks to exhaust mothers because he fears their influence. A weary mother often forgets her worth. Yet when she returns to the Source, her strength is renewed. The nurturing mother learns to rest in the truth that her labor is not unnoticed. "Be not weary in well doing: for in due season ye shall reap, if ye faint not."

Nurture in Sisterhood

Among women, nurture becomes mentorship. A nurturing friend listens with empathy and speaks with truth. She is neither meddlesome nor indifferent. She prays for her sisters when they cannot pray for themselves. Her counsel is not rooted in opinion but in Scripture.

Nurturing sisterhood rebuilds what gossip destroys. It creates safe spaces for repentance and renewal. The nurturing woman sees beyond appearance to the story beneath. She carries the burdens of others with discretion, believing that no wound is wasted when it leads back to God.

When women nurture one another, the church grows in maturity and grace. The younger find guidance; the elder find purpose. Rivalry fades, and unity is restored.

In the house of God, nurture becomes the pulse of revival.

Nurture Toward God

The highest form of nurture is devotion. Just as a gardener tends soil, the believer must tend her heart before God. Faith does not grow accidentally; it must be cultivated through prayer, worship, and obedience.

To nurture one's walk with God is to daily return to His Word, to water the soul with gratitude, and to guard against the weeds of distraction. It means slowing down to listen when the Spirit speaks, allowing silence to become sanctuary.

When a woman nurtures her relationship with God, all other forms of nurture flourish naturally. Her patience deepens because she has lingered in His presence.

Her compassion grows because she has received mercy. Her wisdom strengthens because she abides in truth.

The woman who tends her faith will never lack fruit. Though seasons change and trials come, her roots hold firm in grace. She becomes a tree planted by rivers of living water, bringing forth fruit in her season.

Nurture builds hearts; support steadies them. The same love that teaches must also uphold. As the heart learns to give, it must learn to stand beside.

The Wife and Mother God Calls for This Hour
ELIZABETH ANN SETON

"Train up a child in the way he should go: and when he is old, he will not depart from it."
— Proverbs 22:6

Elizabeth Ann Seton was born into privilege, yet she learned early that true inheritance lies not in wealth but in faith. Raised in New York City in the late eighteenth century, she lived through a time of revolution, rebuilding, and spiritual hunger. Her father was a physician; her mother died when Elizabeth was young. Even in that early sorrow, she began to sense that nurturing others was the surest way to heal her own heart.

As a young wife and mother of five, Elizabeth's home became her sanctuary of service. She loved her husband, William, deeply and devoted herself to their children's education and faith. When William's business failed and his health began to falter, she followed him across the sea to Italy in search of recovery. Instead, she found widowhood. There, surrounded by Catholic friends who tended her grief with gentleness, Elizabeth's faith deepened and changed. She saw in their devotion a love that shaped every part of life; a love that did not separate prayer from practice, or faith from family.

Returning to America as a young widow, she faced loneliness, poverty, and suspicion. Yet within that hardship, God kindled purpose. She began teaching to provide for her children, gathering small groups of students in her home. The work of nurture became her ministry. Her lessons were not only of reading and writing but of reverence and gratitude. She taught that the pursuit of knowledge without the fear of God was hollow, and that the classroom could become a chapel when filled with love.

As word spread of her grace and perseverance, others were drawn to her example. Her faith matured into mission. With a few devoted companions, she founded the Sisters of Charity; the first community of religious women established in America. Together, they opened schools, orphanages, and hospitals. What began as one mother's attempt to raise her own children in truth grew into a movement that would educate generations.

MOTHER OF FAITH AND LEARNING

Elizabeth's nurture was never confined to motherhood alone. Her letters reveal a heart that longed to see every child, rich or poor, learn to read, to pray, and to hope. She believed that every soul was a seed of eternity and that to cultivate the mind was to prepare the spirit for heaven. Her work became the foundation of Catholic education in America, but her spirit of nurture transcended denomination. She saw teaching as an act of love and service as the highest form of learning.

When she was canonized in 1975 as the first native-born saint of the United States, it was not because she lived without sorrow, but because she turned sorrow into sanctification. Her life teaches that nurture is not sentiment; it is sacrifice offered in joy. It is the willingness to stay near when others leave, to teach when the world forgets, to believe that every child, every home, every heart can still become holy ground.

Elizabeth Ann Seton reminds us that nurture begins not in strength but in surrender. Her classrooms were small, her means limited, yet her faith multiplied them. She turned motherhood into ministry and education into evangelism. The seeds she planted in her lifetime continue to bloom in schools and homes across the nation.

Through her story, we remember that the truest form of nurture is to teach others how to love God. It is to shape minds that will one day shape nations. Her legacy endures because she understood this truth: when love instructs, learning becomes worship

Reflection Questions

Where in my home or relationships am I called to nurture rather than control?

How do I speak life into those I love, even when I feel unseen?

What habits of prayer could renew the atmosphere of my household?

How can I cultivate the gifts of others without comparing them to my own?

Prayer for Nurture

Father of Mercy,

Teach me to love patiently and to serve joyfully. Let my words be seasoned with grace and my hands guided by wisdom.

Guard my heart from hardness and my speech from haste. Help me to see those around me through Thy eyes.

May my home become a garden where Thy peace may dwell. Strengthen me when I am weary and remind me that no act of care is forgotten.

Let every meal prepared, every lesson taught, every tear wiped become an offering to Thee. In the quiet work of nurture, let Thy Spirit be glorified.

In the name of Jesus Christ, Amen.

ELIZABETH ANN SETON AND CHAPTER 19

CHAPTER 20

Supportiveness: Standing Beside With Peace and Respect

"*Two are better than one; because they have a good reward for their labour.*"

— ECCLESIASTES 4:9

SUPPORTIVENESS

Supportiveness is strength given quietly, not attention demanded loudly. Supportiveness is not a lesser strength; it is love given structure. It is the art of holding steady what God has built and encouraging what He is growing. In a world that glorifies independence, support has been mistaken for weakness. Yet heaven measures greatness not by how high one climbs, but by how faithfully one upholds.

The woman of God learns that strength and submission are not rivals. The same spirit that bows before the Lord also stands firm beside those He has called her to love. Her presence steadies others because her peace comes from within. She does not enable sin or silence truth, but she chooses gentleness over grievance, harmony over hostility.

Supportiveness is a ministry of alignment. It means to come alongside God's order and lift, not to resist it or remake it. Where the world teaches competition, Scripture teaches companionship. "Bear ye one another's burdens, and so fulfil the law of Christ." The supportive woman sees life not as a contest but as covenant. She knows that to strengthen another is to strengthen the whole.

The counterfeit of supportiveness is self-promotion; the constant striving to be seen, validated, or praised. The supportive woman does not live for applause. Her reward is peace. She trusts that what she builds in secret, God Himself will sustain.

Support begins in the heart, where humility replaces pride and encouragement becomes second nature. It is not flattery, nor is it passivity. True support corrects with honor and uplifts with discernment. It steadies the weary and restores the willing. To support well is to love well.

Support in Marriage

In marriage, support is the soil of unity. A supportive wife does not echo every emotion nor resist every decision. She anchors her husband with trust and steadies him through faith. Her strength is not found in dominance, but in devotion. She does not control by fear or by silence, but by quiet constancy.

The world mocks submission as subservience, yet God calls it spiritual strength. Submission in marriage is not servitude; it is partnership guided by peace. The supportive wife sees her husband not as competitor but as co-laborer in grace. She prays for his discernment, celebrates his victories, and guards his reputation when others would criticize.

Support in marriage is expressed in both word and presence. She learns when to speak and when to stay still. Her counsel becomes trusted because it is anchored in Scripture, not emotion. When she honors her husband, she strengthens his courage. When she believes in him, she multiplies his faith.

Her love is not blind, but believing. It sees what could be if grace continues its work. Her quiet faith becomes a shelter in storm and a mirror of God's patience. Many homes have been restored not by debate but by the gentle consistency of a wife who refused to lose her peace.

Support in Motherhood

Supportiveness in motherhood is the posture of coming alongside rather than hovering above. It means guiding without grasping, teaching without controlling. Children flourish when they feel both secure and trusted. A supportive mother gives boundaries that lead toward freedom, not fear.

When her children stumble, she steadies without shame. When they succeed, she celebrates without envy. She does not compare her children to others; she prays them into their own purpose. Her goal is not perfection but perseverance. The supportive mother walks beside, not ahead, allowing God to lead them both.

Her home is not a stage for performance but a workshop for growth. In moments of correction, her tone carries grace; in moments of celebration, her joy carries humility. She knows that her role will change through seasons, but her presence remains their constant peace.

Supportive motherhood models divine patience. It teaches children that failure is not the end of love and that obedience is not the loss of self. The strength of her faith becomes their foundation. She reminds them that no matter how far they go, they were never meant to walk alone.

Support in Sisterhood

Among women, supportiveness is often tested. The enemy loves to turn companions into competitors, replacing fellowship with comparison. Yet when women choose support over rivalry, the world witnesses redemption in motion.

Supportive sisterhood is rooted in mutual respect. It celebrates the calling of another without feeling threatened. It rejoices when others rise and reaches out when they fall. The supportive woman does not gossip about her sisters; she guards their honor as she would her own. Her encouragement becomes refuge.

When a friend succeeds, she praises God with her. When a sister struggles, she kneels beside her. Her counsel is gentle but firm, guiding others back toward truth. She builds confidence not through praise alone, but through prayerful honesty.

Supportive women multiply hope. Their unity restores what division has destroyed. Together, they remind the world that faith still flourishes when women walk in grace.

Support Toward God

The greatest support a woman offers is the one she gives to heaven's will. Support toward God means agreement with His truth even when it contradicts her feelings. It is a posture of faith that says, "Not my will, but Thine be done."

Supporting the will of God requires surrender and steadfastness. It is easy to cheer when life feels ordered, but true support is proven in surrender. When prayers seem unanswered, the supportive heart does not accuse; it abides. She chooses reverence over resentment.

This kind of faith holds the line when circumstances shake. It trusts that God's design for authority, timing, and order is good. The supportive woman carries a quiet strength born of submission. Her worship is steady, not situational. She praises through trial and obeys without delay.

Her greatest testimony is not what she builds but what she upholds. Like pillars in a temple, her faith holds the weight of what others lean upon. She reminds the world that to stand beside God's purpose is the truest form of power.

Support strengthens unity; hospitality shares it. What begins as peace within the home extends outward into welcome for others.

THE WIFE AND MOTHER GOD CALLS FOR THIS HOUR

PRISCILLA

"A certain Jew named Apollos... was instructed in the way of the Lord; and being fervent in the spirit... he began to speak boldly in the synagogue: whom when Aquila and Priscilla had heard, they took him unto them, and expounded unto him the way of God more perfectly." — ACTS 18:24–26

Priscilla and her husband Aquila were tentmakers by trade and disciples by calling. They lived during a turbulent time for the early church, when persecution scattered believers across the Roman world. Yet wherever they went, Corinth, Ephesus, Rome; the church took root in their home. Together, they built not only a shelter for travelers but a spiritual refuge for saints.

Priscilla's support was not silent; it was steadfast. She stood beside her husband in ministry, teaching, and hospitality. When Apollos, a learned man mighty in Scripture, arrived preaching an incomplete gospel, Priscilla and Aquila invited him into their home. With gentleness and wisdom, they instructed him more perfectly in the truth of Christ. From that meeting came a teacher who would strengthen churches across the Mediterranean.

Their table became more than a place of food, it was a place of formation. As Priscilla explained the Scriptures, she taught with the steadiness of one who had first been taught by grace. She understood that truth, when spoken in love, does not humiliate; it heals.

Her example reveals that supportiveness is not passivity but partnership. She was neither behind her husband nor above him, but beside him, working, reasoning, praying. Her faith gave stability to their home and credibility to their ministry. Together, they modeled unity that defied the culture of their age.

When Paul wrote to the Corinthians and Romans, he mentioned their names with honor, calling them "my helpers in Christ Jesus." Their ministry had saved his life more than once. Such recognition was not born of prominence but of constancy.

COUNSELOR OF THE CHURCH

Priscilla and Aquila used what they had: a home, a trade, and a willing heart to uphold the church.

Through Priscilla, we see that support is not small work. It is the scaffolding upon which truth is built. Every act of hospitality, every prayer whispered for a leader, every word of counsel given in love carries eternal weight. She teaches us that those who stand beside righteousness are as vital as those who stand before crowds.

Her story invites every woman to see her place of influence not as lesser but as luminous. The kingdom of God advances not through competition but throgh cooperation. When women support one another in faith, truth travels farther and endures longer. Priscilla's legacy remains wherever believers open their homes, teach truth together, and strengthen the weary for the work of the gospel.

Every woman who mentors with humility, every wife who strengthens her husband's work, every believer who opens her home for truth to dwell follows in Priscilla's steps. Her legacy endures wherever faith is taught, not through pride, but through partnership.

Reflection Questions

How do I strengthen those I love without seeking recognition?

Where in my relationships might support mean quiet prayer instead of persuasion?

What voices do I amplify, and do they draw others closer to God or to myself?

How can I become a source of steadiness in moments of conflict or doubt?

Prayer for Support

Lord of Peace,

Teach me to stand beside others with grace and courage. Let my words heal rather than wound, and my presence bring calm where there is unrest.

Make my heart a refuge for those who struggle and a strength to those who lead. Deliver me from pride and the need for praise. Help me to uphold others without losing sight of Thee.

Where I am tempted to control, teach me to trust. Where I am weary of giving, renew my joy in service. May my support reflect Thy steadfast love and strengthen Thy kingdom on earth.

In the name of Jesus Christ, Amen.

CHAPTER 21

Order in the Home and Heart

"god is not the author of confusion, but of peace." — 1 corinthians 14 : 33

ORDER IN THE HOME AND HEART

Order is the quiet language of trust. It is what happens when a heart submitted to Christ begins to shape its surroundings after His peace. A woman of order does not chase perfection or appearances; she longs for alignment; a life arranged around what God says matters most.

Order is not the stiffness of control but the softness of communion.
It is the posture that says:
"My home, my time, and my spirit belong to the Lord."

Every space tended, every task completed, every rhythm established becomes worship when it flows from love. Disorder grows where faith forgets its center—where fear scatters focus, where worry multiplies noise, where busyness steals the stillness needed to hear God's voice. Yet the Lord gently calls His daughters back to simplicity.

Order is not punishment; it is protection.
It guards joy from being drowned in distraction and keeps truth from being buried under clutter, both physical and spiritual. When we yield our time and home to God's wisdom, beauty follows. Chaos may knock, but it cannot stay long in a house governed by peace.

A woman of order understands that holiness is expressed in the smallest details. How she keeps her table. How she keeps her thoughts. How she keeps her temper. All of these become quiet offerings to God.

Order restores clarity of calling. When priorities are rightly placed, love regains its strength. The woman of order begins her day by seeking God's sequence: worship before work, gratitude before goals, presence before pressure. Her alignment becomes the evidence that peace is possible in a restless world.

Order in Marriage

Order in marriage begins with shared rhythm—two hearts anchored to one God. It is the consistent, gentle discipline of honoring covenant through daily choices, small habits, and thoughtful words.

An ordered wife does not demand that life follow her design; she asks that love follow God's. She speaks with intention, listens with patience, and keeps grace woven into the routines that hold her home together.

Time becomes her ally rather than her tyrant. She creates rhythms that nourish union: Moments for devotion, evenings for rest, space for conversation, boundaries around noise and weariness.

These quiet safeguards sanctify the ordinary and keep unity from being neglected.

In conflict, she refuses to let chaos lead the way. She returns to prayer, allows humility to soften her tone, and keeps reconciliation within reach. Her attitude becomes the thermostat of the home; steadying what could divide, warming what might grow cold.

True order in marriage is humility arranged into harmony. It is the willingness to keep God first, each other second, and self last. This alignment invites heaven's music into earthly love, transforming routines into blessings and covenant into joy.

She also remembers that order requires continual forgiveness. No marriage can remain in rhythm when resentment piles up like clutter. The ordered wife practices quick repentance, gentle restoration, and a heart ready to begin again. Peace protected daily is a greater gift than apologies offered rarely.

Order in Motherhood

Order in motherhood is the gift of rhythm; creating a home that shapes children not through pressure, but through peace. It is the steady structure that gives them security, the predictable boundaries that help them flourish, and the joyful routines that prepare their hearts to hear God.

An ordered mother does not aim to control every outcome; she creates an environment where growth is possible. She teaches her children that home is a place where love has shape, where days have meaning, and where responsibilities are shared with gladness.

Order turns chaos into clarity: Morning routines that begin with gratitude, spaces that invite creativity rather than overwhelm, schedules that leave room for rest, reading, and wonder, correction given with calm, not haste.

When children stumble, she offers steadiness rather than shame. When they succeed, she celebrates with humility. She does not compare her children with others; she forms them with intention, praying them toward the purpose God has for them.

Order in motherhood is the quiet discipline that says, "Peace lives here."
It teaches obedience without harshness, responsibility without panic, and delight without disruption. It forms children who know, deeply, that their home is a shelter built by faith.

Order in Sisterhood

Among women, the first disorder often comes through comparison. The enemy loves to replace unity with envy, fellowship with competition. But a woman of godly order guards her relationships with intentional peace.

She arranges her friendships around truth, honor, and mutual uplift. She celebrates the victories of others without feeling diminished. She speaks encouragement rather than criticism. She sets boundaries where gossip might creep in and replaces insecurity with blessing.

Order in sisterhood is the commitment to keep the heart free of clutter; the clutter of jealousy, rivalry, or hidden resentment. She protects unity by choosing love over pride, understanding over assumption, prayer over complaint.

When a sister rises, she rejoices. When one falls, she kneels beside her. Her ordered heart creates space for others to breathe and belong.

Order Toward God
The highest form of order is obedience—placing God first and everything else beneath His Lordship.

Order toward God is agreement with His design, His timing, His authority. It is the posture that says, "Your way is best, even when mine feels easier."

An ordered woman refuses to let spiritual chaos rule her inner world. She carves out time to pray, even when life feels loud. She anchors her day in Scripture, knowing that without God's Word her heart drifts. She aligns her decisions with heaven's wisdom, not her impulses.

Her worship is steady, not situational.
Her reverence shapes her routine.
Her surrender brings her into sequence with the Kingdom.

This is the order that builds a legacy; a life where the presence of God is welcomed, where His peace rests on every decision, and where her home becomes a quiet testimony of what happens when Christ is the center of everything.

The Wife and Mother God Calls for This Hour

LAURA INGALLS WILDER

"It is the sweet, simple things of life which are the real ones after all." — LAURA INGALLS WILDER

Laura Ingalls Wilder grew up in a world where order was survival. Her earliest memories were of wind-swept prairies, bitter winters, and the endless work that kept a pioneer family alive.

In a single day, her father could face the loss of a crop, her mother the danger of isolation, and the children the challenge of learning by firelight. Yet within that rugged landscape, Laura's family built not only homes, but harmony. Their faith, discipline, and gratitude kept their hearts from drifting into despair.

Born in 1867, Laura was the second daughter of Charles and Caroline Ingalls. Her parents taught her that outer order was the reflection of inner peace. Each morning began with work, prayer, and a sense of purpose. In their small cabin on the frontier, everything had its place and every life its rhythm. Pa's fiddle filled the nights with song, Ma's hands brought order from chaos, and the children learned that diligence was its own reward.

Laura never forgot those lessons. She learned that the difference between hardship and happiness often came down to the spirit in which one faced it. The prairie could be cruel; fires, storms, and hunger visited often, but her parents' calm steadiness transformed trial into training. "If wisdom's ways you wisely seek," her mother would say, "five things observe with care: of whom you speak, to whom you speak, and how, and when, and where."

As she grew, Laura carried that quiet order into her own life. Marriage to Almanzo Wilder brought new hardships: failed crops, illness, and loss of their first child, but also the joy of shared endurance. She kept faith through rhythm: work, prayer, gratitude. The Wilders' little farmhouse became a symbol of resilience built on divine order.

Years later, as the world changed and the memory of the pioneers began to fade, Laura turned to writing. At first, she wrote for local newspapers, encouraging women to

ORDER ON THE FRONTIER

find beauty in simplicity and moral strength in duty. Her words echoed the same conviction she had learned as a girl: that a well-kept home was not vanity, but virtue. It was the outer fruit of an inner faith.

Her famous Little House books grew out of those convictions. They were not mere nostalgia, they were instruction. Through her stories, she reminded generations that order is not the enemy of freedom; it is what makes freedom flourish. She wrote of family routines, of quiet evenings by lamplight, of prayer said before bread was broken. Beneath every tale of prairie life lay a truth: that the human heart finds peace when it learns to live by God's rhythm.

Laura's writing never glorified comfort. She wrote of hunger, sickness, and loss with honesty, yet always returned to gratitude. Her faith was woven not in grand gestures, but in small obedience: the morning chore done well, the prayer spoken before sleep, the grace said before meals. These were her acts of worship. Her life taught that when the heart is ordered by faith, even hardship can be holy.

In her later years, as she looked back on the decades of change and toil, Laura saw that her family's greatest inheritance was not land or legacy but perspective. She once said, "Home is the nicest word there is." For her, order was not control; it was contentment, the peace that comes from knowing where one's strength begins and where God's sovereignty completes it.

Laura Ingalls Wilder's story endures because it reminds us that the world may shift, but divine order never changes. Her pioneer life stands as a parable for every woman who longs for balance in a restless age. The same faith that steadied her wagon on the plains can steady our homes today.

Through her, we learn that true order is not about perfection, it is about peace. It is choosing gratitude over grumbling, simplicity over striving, worship over worry. Her legacy invites us to look again at our own homes and hearts and to remember that when God reigns within, every humble space can become a sanctuary.

Reflection Questions

What areas of my home or heart reveal disorder that mirrors distraction from God?

Which possessions or patterns quietly steal peace from my family's rhythm?

How can I use time as a covenant offering instead of a personal resource?

What would it look like today to let God reorder my priorities toward peace?

Prayer for Order

Lord of Harmony,

Teach me to keep my home and heart in Thy peace. Let my thoughts be still before Thee and my hands be guided by grace.

Deliver me from the unrest of comparison and the noise of excess. Where confusion has gathered, bring clarity; where hurry has taken root, restore holy rhythm.

Help me to value time as Thy gift and to use it with gratitude. May my home reflect the calm of heaven and my days unfold in Thy design.

When disorder tempts me to despair, remind me that peace begins within. Let every room I tend and every hour I redeem become an offering to Thee.

In the name of Jesus Christ, Amen.

CHAPTER 22

Hospitality: The Home As Refuge and Ministry

*"*BE *not forgetful to entertain strangers: for thereby some have entertained angels unawares." — HEBREWS 13:2*

HOSPITALITY

Hospitality is holiness expressed through welcome. Hospitality is the open door of the Gospel. It is the practice of turning ordinary spaces into sacred ground. In every generation, the faithful have carried light into darkness not only through sermons and songs, but through meals shared, beds offered, and kindness given to the weary.

True hospitality is not performance; it is presence. It does not require perfect homes or unblemished tables. It requires hearts willing to see people as God sees them. The woman who welcomes others welcomes the work of heaven. When she opens her door, she opens her heart, and in doing so she invites God to dwell there.

The world has reduced hospitality to decoration and entertainment. It prizes display over devotion and perfection over peace. Yet in Scripture, hospitality was an act of courage and covenant. It was the difference between isolation and community, between despair and redemption. Abraham's tent became an altar because he received strangers with reverence. Lydia's home became a church because she received the apostles with faith.

The pattern remains: homes that welcome God's people become homes where God moves. Hospitality begins not in the kitchen, but in the heart. It is the posture of availability; of being willing to serve whoever God sends. It is compassion with a face and faith with hands. To practice hospitality is to proclaim that the world may be cold, but love still burns within.

The counterfeit of hospitality is performance. It seeks approval rather than a relationship. The hostess who entertains to impress may please guests for an evening, but the one who serves to bless leaves eternal warmth. The table of hospitality is not set for applause but for communion.

Hospitality in Marriage

Hospitality in marriage begins with the spirit of welcome between husband and wife. A home cannot offer peace to others if it does not first dwell in unity within. A hospitable marriage is one where both partners create an atmosphere of kindness, grace, and respect.

When a wife greets her husband not with reproach but with warmth, she mirrors the grace of Christ who receives His own joyfully. Her home becomes his sanctuary from the noise of the world. When she invites her husband into conversation and care, she welcomes partnership rather than pressure.

Hospitality in marriage extends beyond open doors to open hearts. It means forgiving quickly, speaking gently, and protecting the peace that others will soon feel when they enter. Every guest who crosses the threshold senses whether love lives there. A hospitable wife tends that love carefully, knowing that every word spoken in private echoes in the spirit of her home.

Hospitality in Motherhood

Hospitality in motherhood transforms routine into ministry. A mother welcomes not only guests, but her own children; day after day, meal after meal, question after question. She learns that to receive them with joy is to receive Christ Himself.

When she creates space for conversation at the table, she teaches belonging. When she listens without haste, she teaches compassion. When she keeps her home in gentle order, she teaches reverence for the life God has given. Her hospitality is not decoration but discipleship.

A mother's hospitality also teaches her children how to treat others. They learn generosity not through instruction but through imitation. When they see her serve guests with gladness, they see the heart of God at work. In time, they too will open their homes because they first felt welcome in hers.

The most lasting hospitality is not extended to strangers but practiced daily among family. It is the tone of voice, the smile across the room, the warmth that restores confidence and peace. The children who grow up in such a home carry that grace wherever they go.

Hospitality in Sisterhood

Hospitality among women turns competition into community. It invites one another into the spaces of our lives without fear of judgment. When women open their doors, share their tables, and speak honestly, healing begins.

A hospitable woman does not wait until her home is spotless to invite others in. She opens it in faith, trusting that presence matters more than perfection. In doing so, she builds trust.

Her table becomes a place where burdens are shared and hope is rekindled. Hospitality in sisterhood also means emotional welcome. It is the willingness to make room in one's heart for another's story, to listen without haste, and to offer compassion without comparison. It creates friendship that is rooted not in convenience but in covenant love.

When women gather in prayer, in laughter, or in quiet conversation, they practice the kind of hospitality that knits the body of Christ together. They remind one another that we are not alone in the work of faith or in the weight of life.

Hospitality Toward God

Hospitality toward God is the soul's readiness to receive Him. It is the inner life swept clean and the heart made room for His presence. Jesus said, "If any man hear My voice and open the door, I will come in to him, and will sup with him."

To be hospitable toward God is to keep a home where He is always welcome. It is to set aside time for prayer, to prepare the heart for worship, and to live in such a way that His Spirit feels at rest within us. When we clear the clutter of sin and hurry, we make space for holiness.

The woman who practices divine hospitality lives in constant invitation. Her home is peaceful because her soul is not crowded. She welcomes correction as readily as blessing, knowing both are gifts from a loving Father. Her prayer each morning is simple: "Abide with me."

When she welcomes God, she learns how to welcome others. His presence in her life becomes the fragrance of her home. Those who enter may not understand what they sense, but they feel peace, and peace always preaches.

Hospitality opens the door; peacekeeping keeps it open. The love that welcomes must also protect the harmony that follows.

The Wife and Mother God Calls for This Hour
THE SHUNAMMITE WOMAN

"LET us make a little chamber, I pray thee, on the wall; and let us set for him there a BED, and a table, and a stool, and a candlestick." — 2 KINGS 4:10

The Shunammite woman lived in a small town in Israel during the ministry of Elisha. Scripture calls her "a great woman," not because of wealth or reputation, but because of discernment and devotion. When she perceived that Elisha was a man of God, she persuaded her husband to offer him a meal whenever he passed through.

Her table soon became a refuge for a weary prophet, and her hospitality became the beginning of a miracle. Her kindness did not end at the table. Desiring to make her welcome permanent, she said to her husband, "Let us make a little chamber on the wall." Together they built a quiet room furnished with only what was needful; a bed, a table, a stool, and a candlestick. It was simple, yet holy. They made space not just for a guest, but for the presence of God that traveled with him.

Elisha, moved by her generosity, asked what he might do for her. She asked for nothing. Her contentment was her testimony. But the prophet saw what her heart had buried, years of longing for a child. He spoke the promise that by the next season, she would embrace a son. The child was born, and joy filled her home.

Years later, that same child fell sick and died in her arms. In grief, she carried him to the prophet's chamber, laid him on the bed she had prepared, and went in search of Elisha. Her words were steady: "It shall be well." She returned with the man of God, and before the day ended, her son breathed again. The same room she built for ministry became the place of resurrection.

The Shunammite's hospitality gave God room to move. Her story teaches that when we prepare space for holiness, heaven fills it. She did not entertain for gain or recognition; she built for presence. The simplicity of her offering invited miracles.

Her table fed the servant of God; her upper room raised the next generation. Her example calls every woman to see her home as a sanctuary. A meal offered in love, a chair pulled

MAKING ROOM FOR THE PROPHET

close in conversation, a room opened to prayer; all become holy acts when given to God. True hospitality is not what we show others, but what we give Him through others.

Even now, the spirit of the Shunammite lives wherever women choose to open their homes in faith. Her legacy reminds us that hospitality is not about comfort; it is about covenant. When we make room for the things of God, He makes room for the impossible.

Reflection Questions

How can I make my home a place of peace rather than performance?

What hinders me from welcoming others as freely as I should?

In what ways can my table or conversation become ministry?

How can I invite God's presence more intentionally into my home?

Prayer for Hospitality

Lord of Welcome,

Enter the rooms of my heart and make them Thine. Teach me to open my door without hesitation and my hands without fear.

Let every meal shared, every guest received, every word spoken at my table become worship unto Thee. Guard me from pride in presentation and grant me joy in presence.

May my home reflect Thy kindness and my life reveal Thy peace. When others enter, let them find not perfection but Thy presence. Fill my home, O Lord, until it feels like heaven's threshold.

In the name of Jesus Christ, Amen.

Making Room for the Prophet and chapter 22

CHAPTER 23

Peacekeeping: Calming Conflict and Protecting Joy

"BLESSED *are the peacemakers: for they shall be called the children of God.*" — MATTHEW 5:9

PEACEKEEPING

Peacekeeping is courage clothed in gentleness. It is not the absence of conflict, but the art of bringing calm where chaos seeks control. The peacekeeper is not weak or timid; she is anchored. Her heart is ruled by the Prince of Peace, and wherever she walks, His spirit follows.

In every generation, God calls women to be builders of peace—within homes, among sisters, in communities, and before Him. The work is quiet yet powerful. It requires patience that refuses to retaliate and faith that believes God can heal what anger has divided.

Peace does not come naturally to the fallen heart. It must be practiced, prayed for, and protected. The enemy delights in discord. He thrives in noise and misunderstanding, whispering pride where humility should dwell. But the woman who guards her peace guards her home. She knows that the atmosphere she permits will one day become the atmosphere her children carry.

To keep peace is to stand between heaven and earth, reminding the world that reconciliation is possible. The peacekeeper does not need to win; she needs to restore.

Her words become balm rather than a weapon. Her silence is not avoidance but discernment. And her forgiveness is not weakness; it is worship.

Peacekeeping in Marriage

Peace in marriage begins when both hearts rest under God's authority. It cannot be forced through argument or maintained through fear. It grows in the soil of grace and mutual honor. A peacekeeping wife does not mirror irritation; she models restraint. When tension rises, she chooses prayer over pride and gentleness over retaliation.

The world rewards dominance, yet heaven rewards humility. A peaceful home is not one where no voice is raised, but where every word is redeemed. The peacekeeping wife learns to listen fully before she speaks. She sows calm through kindness, remembering that she cannot change her husband's heart but can guard her own.

When frustration comes, she steps back into the presence of God before reentering the conversation. Her composure softens her husband's spirit. Over time, peace becomes their language. The home once strained by competition becomes a place of cooperation. The marriage ruled by Christ becomes a witness to others that love can still dwell in patience.

Peacekeeping in Motherhood

Peacekeeping in motherhood is the steady pulse of calm that quiets a child's world. It is the gentle word when tempers flare and the measured tone that brings order to chaos. Children learn emotional safety not through perfection, but through a mother's peaceful consistency.

The peacekeeping mother teaches that disagreement need not destroy relationship. She models apology, restores harmony after correction, and guards her children's hearts from resentment. She prays that her home will be a sanctuary where laughter outlasts conflict and forgiveness follows quickly.

When storms rise, whether between siblings or within herself; she returns to stillness. Her calm is contagious. Her restraint teaches strength. Her peace becomes their confidence.

Many children grow up remembering not their mother's words but her presence. When that presence carried peace, they carried it into their own homes.

Peacekeeping in Sisterhood

Among women, peacekeeping becomes a ministry of reconciliation. Words have power to divide or to heal. The peacekeeping woman refuses to spread rumor or fan resentment. She chooses to speak life. When offense comes, she seeks clarity before complaint, and prayer before participation.

Peacekeeping in sisterhood restores what gossip destroys. It rebuilds trust where suspicion has lived. A single word of peacemaking can silence an entire storm. The woman of peace values unity more than being right. She listens to understand, not to respond. Her composure disarms contention.

Her presence in a group brings balance. When others rush to take sides, she reminds them to seek truth with grace. The peace she carries is not her own; it flows from time spent with God. The peacekeeper becomes a bridge; steady, unseen, yet strong enough to hold the weight of reconciliation.

Peacekeeping Toward God

True peacekeeping begins within. The woman who guards her heart before God will carry peace wherever she goes. It is impossible to bring calm outwardly if the soul is in turmoil. To keep peace with God is to surrender control and trust His will above our own.

Every fear, every grievance, every impatience must be laid at His feet. The believer who rests in His sovereignty will not be easily shaken by the world. Her faith quiets her spirit, and her spirit quiets her surroundings.

Peace with God is the foundation of peace with others. The woman who communes daily with Him carries heaven's stillness into her home. Her words are softer, her reactions slower, her joy deeper. She becomes an instrument of reconciliation because she herself has been reconciled.

Peace makes room for joy; service makes it shine. What is preserved through calm must now be poured out in gladness.

Peacekeeping and Chapter 23

THE WIFE AND MOTHER GOD CALLS FOR THIS HOUR
FROM MY HEARTH

Let's face it: motherhood is not easy. Wife life is hard. Some days the chores multiply like shadows, the sink is full, and dinner still needs cooking, the calendar asks for one more drive, one more teaching moment, one more bit of motivation when my own has gone missing. The tasks feel like they outnumber me three thousand to one.

In those moments, I have learned to begin small. I pretend the floor is clear and the counters are empty, and then I notice just one toy. I know where it goes. But does my little boy? I call him, take his hand, and let myself remember how precious he is; mine, yes, but first the Lord's. Time is short and holy; I forget that until I slow down enough to see it.

We look at the toy together. When did it first come into our home? What color is it, what shape, what small delight did it once bring? We talk for a minute and then we put it away, together. The work is still work, but it changes in my hands. The one thing becomes two, then three. The room does not transform in an instant, but my heart does, a little. Duty begins to move toward devotion, and what felt like drudgery becomes a lesson in tenderness. "How can we treasure this home," I ask my son, "the way God treasures us?" One step, slow and simple. The song in the work is quiet, but it's there.

Being a wife holds a different weight. Bills wait, laundry calls, errands stretch. It's easy to say, "I have to serve," as though I am pressed down by obligation. But the Spirit keeps teaching me to say, "I get to serve," because everything I touch was given by God. Even when I feel bone-empty, I have enough; enough to offer a small kindness, a quick smile, a warm meal, a clean shirt folded with care. These gestures are not grand, and they are not always noticed. Sometimes they are completely unseen. Still, they are notes in the music of our home; quiet chords of love that steady a man who presides, provides, and protects.

I am his partner. Trust is our currency. If he cannot trust me with the hidden work of love, how can I trust him with the visible weight he carries? So I take one task and give it my best. Then a second, if strength allows. Maybe not all of it today. But some. And

THE SONG IN THE WORK

I ask myself the question I avoid when I'm tired: if God extends daily grace to me, will I extend grace to myself, and to my husband? Service is not only what my hands accomplish; it is what my heart becomes while they do it. The work does not just change the room; it changes me.

On my hardest days the Holy Spirit meets me where the work feels most invisible. He reframes the ordinary: folding a shirt becomes a prayer for the man who will wear it; washing dishes becomes thanksgiving for the mouths that were fed; sweeping becomes a quiet blessing over the feet that run through this house. When I am tempted to resent repetition, He turns it into rhythm. When I want to measure worth by what is seen, He reminds me that Heaven hears the song of hidden faithfulness.

There are moments when I would rather escape; leave the mess, chase a different task, find a louder success. But joy rarely waits at the edge of escape; it grows in the field of offering. It returns when I give the task to God, not because the task changed, but because the Giver re-ordered my heart. "And whatsoever ye do, do it heartily, as to the Lord, and not unto men." In that light, the kitchen becomes a sanctuary, the laundry a liturgy, the errand a hymn. My home becomes the place where worship puts on an apron.

I am still learning. I still rush, complain, and forget to sing. Yet the Lord keeps tuning my heart to gratitude. He shows me how small obediences stack into a steady life. He teaches me that being faithful in the little is how He prepares me for the greater. And when I finally hear it, the faint melody under the motions, I remember: God delights not only in what I produce, but in who I become while I serve.

The work remains, but the song is louder now. Not loud to the world, perhaps, but loud enough for Heaven, and for my home. Duty has become devotion. And the place that once felt like a burden is where God meets me again.

The truest worship is often sung in silence, through hands that serve, feet that stay, and hearts that choose gratitude in the unseen. When the work of life feels ordinary, heaven calls it offering. Every folded garment, every whispered prayer, every unseen act of patience becomes a note in the symphony of devotion.

God does not divide sacred and secular; He redeems the simple until it shines. To find the song in our work is to discover that joy was never lost, it was waiting in the rhythm of faithfulness all along.

Reflection Questions

How do I respond when conflict arises; do I bring calm or fuel the fire?

What practices help me return to peace when emotions pull me away?

Where in my relationships might God be asking me to ride toward reconciliation?

How can my words and silence both become tools of peace?

Prayer for Peacekeeping

God of Still Waters,

Teach me to carry Thy calm into every storm. Let my heart be slow to anger and swift to mercy.

When conflict arises, help me to see beyond pride to purpose. Make my tongue gentle, my thoughts pure, and my spirit patient.

Where there is division, let me sow reconciliation. Where there is fear, let me speak faith.

Where there is unrest, let me carry Thy presence. Fill my home, Lord, with the peace that cannot be shaken, And make me a keeper of joy in every season.

In the name of Jesus Christ, Amen.

THE SONG IN THE WORK AND CHAPTER 23

CHAPTER 24

Joyful Service: Finding Purpose In Duty

"SERVE *the Lord with gladness: come before His presence with singing.*" — PSALM 100:2

Service is the language of love. It is how faith takes form and gratitude becomes visible. The woman of God understands that her daily labors; whether great or small, are opportunities to honor the One who gave her breath. When she serves with joy, her work ceases to be a burden and becomes worship.

The world teaches that joy and duty cannot coexist, that service depletes rather than delights. Yet Scripture reveals the opposite. Joyful service does not drain; it renews. It transforms ordinary moments into sacred exchanges. The woman who sweeps her floor with praise does more for the kingdom than one who seeks applause without obedience.

True service begins with surrender. It asks not, "What must I do?" but "Whom do I serve?" When the answer is Christ, every task is infused with meaning. The heart that delights in duty no longer needs recognition, for it already possesses reward.

The counterfeit of joyful service is resentment. It performs the act but misses the heart. The joyful servant remembers that every act of care, every hidden kindness, every unseen effort is recorded in heaven. She understands that joy is not the absence of effort but the presence of purpose.

Joyful Service in Marriage

In marriage, service is the expression of covenant love. A joyful wife serves not out of obligation but affection. She looks for ways to bless rather than to be noticed. Her care strengthens the bond of unity because it is freely given.

When she prepares a meal, speaks kindly after disagreement, or chooses forgiveness over frustration, she serves both her husband and her Lord. Her service restores what selfishness erodes. She does not keep score, for joy cannot coexist with comparison.

The joyful wife sees her home as ministry. Her hands become instruments of peace, her words instruments of grace. In her quiet acts of love, she preaches the gospel more powerfully than through any argument. The marriage that begins in service often ends in song.

Joyful Service in Motherhood

Joyful service in motherhood transforms monotony into meaning. Each diaper changed, each tear wiped, each story read at bedtime becomes a hymn of devotion.

The mother who serves with gladness does not despise small beginnings; she recognizes that eternity grows in them. Her work may be unseen by the world, but it resounds in heaven. The God who saw Hagar in the wilderness sees every mother who labors in love. The joyful mother guards her attitude more than her schedule, knowing that her children will remember her countenance long after they forget her chores.

When exhaustion threatens to steal her song, she recalls that service is not slavery but sanctification. Every act of care refines her spirit. Through serving her family, she becomes more like Christ, who "came not to be ministered unto, but to minister."

Joyful Service in Sisterhood

Among women, joyful service weaves community. It looks for needs and meets them quietly. It rejoices when others rejoice and bears burdens without complaint. The woman who serves her sisters strengthens the whole household of faith.

In a culture that exalts independence, she chooses interdependence. Her joy is multiplied in giving. Whether she brings a meal to the weary, watches a friend's children, or listens without judgment, she becomes a vessel of comfort.

Her presence reminds others that love still acts. Words may encourage, but service endures. When women serve one another with glad hearts, the church shines again as family.

Joyful Service Toward God

The highest service is rendered to God Himself. Every earthly act of care becomes divine when offered to Him. The woman who serves the Lord with gladness does not separate her chores from her calling. She worships through work and finds Him in the midst of her labor.

Service toward God is not measured by scale but by sincerity. A single prayer whispered while folding clothes can move heaven as surely as a sermon preached from a pulpit. He measures motive more than magnitude. When a woman learns to serve God in the details, her joy becomes indestructible.

Her faith turns duty into delight, and her labor into legacy. The joy of the Lord becomes her strength, and that strength renews the world around her. Service matures into legacy. The work of the hands becomes the inheritance of the heart. What we offer in joy becomes the seed of generations who will serve the Lord with gladness.

The Song in the Work and Chapter 24

The Wife and Mother God Calls for This Hour

CLARA BARTON

"and let us not be weary in well doing: for in due season we shall reap, if we faint not." — galatians 6:9

Clara Barton was born in 1821 on a small Massachusetts farm, the youngest of five children. From her earliest years she carried a heart tuned to the needs of others. When her brother David was injured in a fall, twelve-year-old Clara tended him for nearly two years, day and

night. Long before she became known to the world, she learned the sacred rhythm of service; watching, listening, and staying when others grew tired. Her compassion grew into calling. At a time when women were rarely allowed to work outside the home, Clara became a teacher, then founded one of the first free public schools in New Jersey. Yet her greatest work began during the Civil War, when she saw soldiers bleeding on battlefields with no one to care for them. Refusing to remain behind the safety lines, she began collecting bandages, food, and medicine; anything that might ease their suffering.

She rode into danger where few dared go, nursing the wounded under fire at Antietam, Fredericksburg, and countless other battles. Men called her "the angel of the battlefield." Her presence brought calm where chaos reigned. She prayed over dying soldiers, wrote final letters to their families, and comforted those who lived to fight another day. In her, duty and compassion were not rivals; they were one.

Clara's joy was not in recognition but in usefulness. "I may be compelled to face danger," she said, "but never fear it, so long as I am doing right." Her peace came from obedience, not outcome. She saw every wound she dressed as an offering of worship, service made holy through love. When asked how she endured the exhaustion and horror, she replied, "I could run the risk; it was my duty."

After the war, she continued her service tirelessly, leading the effort to identify missing soldiers and reunite them with their families. She established the Office of Missing

THE NURSE OF THE NATION

Soldiers and personally answered more than 63,000 letters from desperate families searching for loved ones. Her persistence restored not only names, but dignity.

In later years, Clara traveled to Europe, where she encountered the newly founded International Red Cross. Seeing its mission as an extension of Christian mercy, she resolved to bring it to America. Through years of resistance, bureaucracy, and doubt, she pressed on until the American Red Cross was finally established in 1881. Under her leadership it became a refuge in war, flood, and famine; a ministry of relief born from the heart of one woman who believed that compassion was sacred duty.

Clara Barton's life teaches that joyful service is not dependent on ease. Her joy came through endurance, her strength through surrender. She did not wait for ideal conditions; she created sanctuaries in the midst of suffering. Her legacy reminds us that the measure of our service is not how much we give, but how faithfully we give it.

Through her, we see that holiness often wears an apron or a uniform, that ministry may look like tending the wounded or comforting the fearful. She turned battlefield tents into chapels of grace and made service a song the nation still remembers.

Every woman who carries compassion into the broken places of the world walks in her footsteps. Every mother who stays beside a sickbed, every teacher who guides a struggling child, every neighbor who shows mercy to the weary continues her ministry. Clara Barton's life whispers the truth of joyful service: that what is done in love, no matter how small, becomes eternal.

Reflection Questions

Do I serve from love or from expectation?

Where has God called me to serve with more joy than complaint?

How can I turn ordinary work into an act of worship?

What legacy of joyful service am I building for those who will follow?

Prayer for Joyful Service

Lord of Gladness,

Teach me to serve with a song in my heart. Let every task, great or small, become an offering of love.

Deliver me from resentment and fill me with gratitude. Remind me that my labor is not forgotten, my effort not unseen.

Strengthen my hands, lighten my spirit, and renew my joy in duty. May I serve others as Thou hast served me, with humility and delight.

Let my home, my work, and my words reveal Thy kindness. And when my day is done, may I hear Thee say, "Well done."

In the name of Jesus Christ, Amen.

PART V

Legacy and Inheritance

"WE *believe that our family was created specifically for this time.*"
    -OUR FAMILY UNDER GOD COMPACT

CHAPTER 25

Reverence

"o come, let us worship and bow down: let us kneel before the Lord our maker."

— PSALM 95 : 6

REVERENCE

Reverence is not fear that drives us away, but love that draws us close. It is the gentle kneeling of the heart, the quiet acknowledgment that God is both infinite and near. The woman who lives with reverence does not shrink before holiness; she leans into it. She bows not because she must, but because she cannot help but adore.

This sacred awe transforms ordinary life into continual worship. Reverence listens before it speaks and notices before it demands. It moves through the day aware that the same hands that shaped the heavens also shape the moments of home. Every task can become an altar when the heart remembers its Maker.

The call of Psalm 95 is an invitation, not a command. "O come," it says—come with joy, come with humility, come with open hands. Reverence accepts that invitation daily. It sanctifies the simple: the laughter of a child, the glow of morning light, the whisper of prayer rising from weary lips. Such reverence does not retreat from the world but redeems it. It reminds her that she carries holy ground wherever she walks. The more she bows in gratitude, the lighter her burdens feel. The more she worships, the more she sees.

Reverence turns life into liturgy and home into sanctuary.

Reverence in Marriage

Reverence within marriage begins with gratitude for the gift of another soul to walk beside. It is the habit of honoring one's spouse not only in public affection but in private thought. When a wife bows before God each morning, she finds the grace to rise in gentleness toward her husband. Reverence helps her see marriage not as competition for comfort, but as companionship in covenant.

Such reverence changes the tone of speech. It softens correction, quiets complaint, and multiplies kindness. It replaces pride with patience and turns disagreement into dialogue. When she chooses humility over victory, she reflects the love of Christ, who served before He spoke. Her home begins to echo the calm of worship rather than the clamor of control.

The reverent wife remembers that affection is fragile when respect is absent. She speaks to her husband as one created in the image of God and guards her words as prayers. Her courtesy is not formality; it is faith in motion.

Reverence within marriage is not weakness but wisdom. It knows that love cannot flourish without honor. In every season young affection, weary duty, or mature friendship reverence steadies the bond. It teaches husband and wife to bow together before the Lord their Maker, and in that posture, they discover again the joy of belonging first to Him and then to one another.

Reverence in Motherhood

Motherhood is one of the purest expressions of reverence, for it requires daily surrender. Each child entrusted to a mother's care is a reminder that life itself is holy. Reverence looks at a sleeping child and whispers thanks; it looks at a struggling child and whispers prayer. It does not claim ownership but stewardship.

A reverent mother teaches her children to notice God. She points out the beauty of creation, the miracle of forgiveness, and the comfort of Scripture. Her faith is not a lecture but a living rhythm, songs sung in the kitchen, prayers spoken in car rides, peace felt in her embrace.

She models that worship is not confined to Sunday but woven into every breath of the week. When impatience tempts her, reverence steadies her. When fear presses in, she remembers that the same Lord who formed their hearts holds their futures. She kneels often not in defeat but in dependence and in doing so teaches that strength grows where surrender abides.

As the years pass, her reverence becomes their remembrance. Long after they leave her care, her quiet awe lingers. They will recall her patience in trouble, her gratitude in lack, her habit of turning worry into prayer. Through her, they learn that the surest way to rise is first to kneel.

Reverence in Sisterhood

Among women, reverence restores peace. It teaches them to approach one another with gentleness and to listen as if God Himself were speaking through another's story. Reverence sees the image of the Maker in every sister and honors it. It refuses to speak carelessly about those God loves.

A community of reverent women becomes a haven of grace. When they gather, conversation turns toward encouragement rather than comparison. They thank God for one another's gifts instead of competing for notice. Reverence teaches that to celebrate another's blessing is an act of worship, for every good gift comes from the same Father.

Such reverence builds bridges where pride builds walls. It allows truth to travel safely between friends because it is carried in love. A reverent friend is slow to assume, quick to forgive, and steady to pray. Her presence stills storms before they begin, for she walks in the quiet authority of peace.

When women choose reverence in their sisterhood, they restore the beauty of holy friendship. They mirror Mary and Elizabeth, women who blessed rather than envied, who rejoiced together in God's wonders. Such friendship becomes a living invitation to worship, echoing the psalmist's call: "O come, let us worship and bow down."

Reverence Toward God

Reverence toward God is the wellspring from which all other reverence flows. It begins with wonder and ends with worship. The woman who knows her Maker as both sovereign and tender finds safety in surrender. She bows not to lose herself but to be renewed.

This posture of the heart transforms every act into praise. Washing, working, resting; all become ways of saying, "Thou art worthy." Reverence teaches her that she can draw near without fear because grace has already made the way. She learns that to kneel is not to cower but to rest in love too great to stand before.

Every day becomes a cathedral when entered with awe. The reverent woman begins her mornings with gratitude and closes her evenings in peace. She bends before His majesty and rises wrapped in His mercy. Her reverence does not silence her; it sanctifies her. She becomes a quiet reflection of His order and His glory.

Reverence toward God transforms her home into a place of presence. It turns the kitchen table into an altar of gratitude and bedtime prayers into hymns of trust. Her life sings softly, "Come, let us kneel before the Lord our Maker," until even her silence praises Him.

Reverence begins with invitation and ends with intimacy. When we kneel before the Lord our Maker, He lifts us into joy, and our homes become echoes of His holiness. As we move forward, we learn that reverence, once rooted, blossoms into hope, hope that anchors the heart through every storm and lights the way for those who follow.

THE WIFE AND MOTHER GOD CALLS FOR THIS HOUR

ELIZABETH

"THUS hath the Lord dealt with me in the days wherein He looked on me, to take away my REPROACH among men." — LUKE 1 : 25

In a quiet Judean town nestled among olive trees lived Elizabeth, wife of Zacharias the priest. Their marriage was marked by devotion, their days ordered by prayer. Scripture says they were both righteous before God, walking in His commandments blameless. Yet for all their faithfulness, the cradle in their home remained empty. Years lengthened into decades, and the dream of motherhood slipped into the background of her prayers. Still, Elizabeth's faith endured. Her reverence was not proven by prosperity but by perseverance. She loved God for who He was, not only for what He gave.

Each year, as Zacharias took his turn serving in the temple, Elizabeth remained faithful in her quiet ministry at home. She prayed for her neighbors, prepared food for the poor, and lived in a posture of gratitude even as her own heart ached. She did not allow disappointment to sour her devotion. Reverence steadied her, teaching her to see holiness in every season. Even in longing, she found reasons to bless the Lord.

Then came the day when everything changed. As Zacharias stood in the holy place burning incense, the angel Gabriel appeared with a message too wondrous to grasp: their prayers had been heard. They would have a son, and he would go before the Messiah to prepare the way of the Lord. Fear and wonder mingled in Zacharias's heart. His disbelief rendered him silent, but Elizabeth's faith broke forth in praise. When life quickened within her womb, she hid herself for five months, not from shame but from sacred awe. She needed time to ponder the miracle that had unfolded in her own body, to let gratitude settle into stillness.

Those months of seclusion became her sanctuary. She prayed, sang psalms of thanksgiving, and remembered the mercy of God through every movement of new life. Reverence deepened her joy. She marveled that the same God who opened

THE QUIET FAITHFULNESS OF REVERENCE

Sarah's womb in ancient days had remembered her name. She knew that the child she carried was not for her alone but for the fulfillment of promise stretching back through generations.

When her young cousin Mary arrived, carrying within her the Savior Himself, Elizabeth's spirit recognized what eyes could not yet see. The child in her womb leapt for joy, and she was filled with the Holy Ghost. Her voice became prophecy as she blessed Mary and praised the faithfulness of God. "Blessed art thou among women," she cried, "and blessed is the fruit of thy womb." Reverence had opened her perception; awe had become her language. Her home turned into a temple that day, filled with the presence of the Lord.

Months later, when her son was born, the neighbors gathered to celebrate. According to custom, they sought to name him after his father, but Elizabeth stood firm: "Not so; he shall be called John." Her obedience to God's word defied expectation. It was then that Zacharias's speech returned, and his first words were praise. Husband and wife, once silent under sorrow, now lifted their voices together in worship.

Elizabeth's reverence shaped more than her own lifetime. The child she raised would one day cry in the wilderness, calling a nation to repentance. The tenderness and discipline of her faith prepared him to recognize the voice of God when it came again beside the Jordan River. Her quiet awe became his courage, her faith his foundation.

Through Elizabeth, we learn that reverence is not reserved for moments of revelation; it is cultivated in years of waiting. God entrusted her with a miracle because she had already learned to worship without one. Her story reminds every woman that holiness grows in hiddenness, that reverence transforms silence into song, and that no season spent in faith is ever wasted. When she bowed her heart before her Maker, heaven stooped to bless her, and the whole world was changed.

Reflection Questions

Where can I slow my pace this week to notice God's presence more fully?

How does reverence shape the way I speak to those I love?

What daily routines in my home could become moments of worship if I approached them with awe?

How might my quiet example invite others to kneel before the Lord their Maker?

Prayer for Reverence

Lord of Love,

Teach me to draw near with joy and humility. Let my heart bow before Thee in every task and conversation.

Cleanse my speech, calm my thoughts, and fill my home with peace. Help me to notice Thy beauty in ordinary days and to honor Thee in all I do.

May reverence crown my worship and shape my service. When I forget to kneel, remind me that Thou art near and worthy.

Let my life whisper continually, "Come, let us worship and bow down."

In the name of Jesus Christ, Amen.

The Quiet Faithfulness of Reverence and chapter 25

CHAPTER 26

Courage & Example

"BE strong and of a good courage, fear not, nor be afraid of them: for the Lord thy God, He it is that doth go with thee; He will not fail thee, nor forsake thee." — DEUTERONOMY 31 : 6

COURAGE & EXAMPLE

Courage is born in the still places of the soul where fear whispers its warnings and faith answers with trust. It is not the roar of defiance but the calm breath that says, I will obey.

True courage does not rise because danger disappears; it rises because conviction has already chosen its master. Every generation requires hearts that will hold fast when the world trembles. Within a woman's quiet strength lies the endurance that steadies her home and preserves her nation.

The woman who fears God learns to measure her steps by His promises rather than by her comfort. She moves forward, not because she sees the path clearly, but because she knows Who leads it. Her courage is refined through surrender. She does not stand apart from suffering; she stands within it, clothed with grace and guarded by purpose. In her presence others find composure, for faith has taught her that no trial can unmake what God has ordained.

Courage also calls a woman to speak truth when silence would be safer. It gives her the strength to defend what is holy even when culture mocks holiness itself. The courage of a godly woman does not bruise; it blesses. It does not command attention but compels respect. Her words carry the weight of eternity because they are spoken from a heart aligned with heaven.

This virtue is both shield and seed. It shields the weak from despair and plants hope in those who watch her live with steadfast peace. When courage becomes a habit rather than a moment, it shapes the atmosphere of an entire household. A brave mother teaches by example that faith is stronger than fear and that obedience is the highest victory.

Courage in Marriage

Marriage often asks for the kind of courage that no one applauds. It requires the bravery to stay soft when seasons grow hard, to forgive when pride aches for vindication, and to listen when weariness would rather retreat. A courageous wife does not build her confidence on her husband's perfection but on God's providence. She chooses patience as her fortress and humility as her sword. When misunderstanding clouds affection, she waits upon the Lord who mends what human effort cannot.

Courage in marriage is found in small obedience. It lives in the woman who prays when words would wound, who holds her tongue until her heart is right, who believes that God can redeem what she cannot repair. Her quiet faith becomes the evidence of things unseen, proving that love rooted in Christ outlasts every storm.

Sometimes courage means beginning again after disappointment. It means greeting each morning as a new mercy rather than an old regret. A wife who walks in this spirit remembers that her covenant is not sustained by feelings but by grace. She bears witness that steadfast love is the mightiest form of bravery.

The courageous marriage becomes a light to weary households around it. Its endurance proclaims that divine love is not fragile, and its peace testifies that forgiveness is freedom. Such courage turns a home into a sanctuary where both husband and wife are safe to grow, to fail, and to rise again in mercy.

Courage in Motherhood

Motherhood is a lifelong campaign of the heart. Every season calls for courage of a different kind. In early years it takes courage to surrender sleep and self for the sake of nurture. Later, it takes courage to let children step into a world that may not honor what they have been taught. A mother's bravery is often unseen, measured in the prayers she whispers while folding small clothes or waiting up for older souls.

Courage teaches her to discipline without anger, to protect without possession, and to trust God when she cannot trace Him. The mother who walks by faith does not fear what tomorrow may bring because she knows Who holds tomorrow. She understands that her calling is not to control outcomes but to cultivate hearts. Her courage rests in the knowledge that obedience today shapes eternity for her children.

When the world presses its anxieties upon her, she returns to the promises of Scripture. "The righteous shall be in everlasting remembrance." She reminds herself that her labor is not in vain. Her courage becomes contagious, for children learn peace by watching her posture. They see how faith steadies her, and they begin to believe that God can steady them too.

In the end, a mother's courage outlives her presence. Long after her hands have grown still, the echo of her steadfastness resounds through her descendants. Her prayers become unseen walls around her family, and her faith becomes the inheritance no thief can take.

Courage in Sisterhood

Among women, courage is often tested in the choice to love rather than compete. Sisterhood requires hearts that will celebrate another's victory and weep for another's loss. It takes courage to stay when misunderstanding arises, to confront with gentleness, and to forgive without record.

True fellowship is not built upon convenience but upon covenantal grace. A courageous sister is a peacemaker. She steps between conflict and calms it with prayer. She covers faults with mercy rather than gossip, remembering that every tongue can either heal or harm. Her courage protects unity because she treasures what God treasures: the bond of peace.

This kind of bravery is refined through humility. To prefer another's good above one's own is not weakness but wisdom. It requires the quiet confidence that God sees every unseen sacrifice.

Courageous sisterhood turns competition into compassion and comparison into gratitude. In a generation marked by isolation, brave women become bridges. They create places where hearts may be honest and still be held. Their loyalty restores trust to communities wounded by betrayal. Such courage within sisterhood reminds the world that the family of faith is not an idea but a living body held together by love.

Courage Toward God

Every other form of courage flows from this one. The woman who fears the Lord finds freedom from all other fears. Courage toward God is born of reverence. It bows before His majesty and rises secure in His mercy. This is the courage of surrender, the bravery of trust. It teaches the soul to obey even when understanding has not yet arrived.

Such courage confesses sin quickly and follows swiftly. It believes that obedience is the safest path, no matter how narrow. It refuses to let delay masquerade as wisdom. The heart that has learned to yield completely to God stands unshaken before man, for its allegiance has already been decided.

In prayer, the courageous woman learns to wait without despair. She believes that God's silence is not absence but preparation. Her faith becomes the still river that runs beneath the changing tides of circumstance. Because she trusts Him, she can face tomorrow without trembling.

To walk courageously before God is to live every day in holy expectancy. It is to greet each trial as an opportunity to glorify Him and each victory as proof of His faithfulness. When her life ends, heaven will call her brave, for she believed that the Lord her God was with her wherever she went.

Courage that begins in the heart of one faithful soul becomes the inheritance of many. What we dare in obedience today becomes the story our children remember tomorrow.

THE WIFE AND MOTHER GOD CALLS FOR THIS HOUR

AMELIA EARHART

"THE most difficult thing is the decision to act; the rest is merely tenacity."
— AMELIA EARHART

When the world still believed that women were made for narrow paths, Amelia Earhart looked toward the sky. From the first time she saw an airplane lift from the earth, she felt a pull that words could not explain; a summons to rise above fear and expectation. Her courage was not reckless; it was reverent. She stood before creation with wonder, certain that the same God who formed the heavens had placed within her the desire to explore them.

Amelia's early life gave her little reason to believe she would one day make history. She was a quiet child, curious and determined, often found with her nose in a book or her hands building small experiments. Her parents' lives were unsettled, their home shifting from place to place, but the instability only strengthened her resolve. She learned to rely on discipline, faith, and the steady voice within that said, "Go forward." Each difficulty became another flight lesson in perseverance.

When she first took to the air as a young woman, the sensation felt less like discovery and more like remembrance, as if her soul already knew what it meant to soar. Yet the courage that lifted her off the ground was not pride but purpose. She saw flight as more than adventure; it was a way to prove that the boundaries placed upon women were false. She wanted to show that courage, intelligence, and endurance were not gifts reserved for men but reflections of the divine image within all who believe they are capable of more.

The world soon took notice. Her record-breaking flights carried her across oceans and continents, but her greatest victories were unseen. She wrote letters to young girls urging them to dream with discipline. She spoke to crowds about bravery and humility, reminding them that risk without faith is folly, but faith without courage accomplishes little. She believed that action born from conviction is the truest form of worship.

THE QUIET COURAGE TO SOAR

Amelia's courage was quiet, steady, and deeply moral. She was never boastful of her fame nor careless with her influence. Her journals reveal a woman of reflection; one who sought meaning even in solitude. "Everyone has oceans to fly," she wrote, "if they have the heart to do it." For her, courage meant more than daring; it meant obedience to calling. Every flight was an act of gratitude for the mind God gave her, the freedom her nation allowed, and the opportunities her faith inspired her to steward well.

In 1937, as she prepared for her final journey to circle the globe, Amelia approached the task not as conquest but as communion with purpose. Friends warned her of danger, yet she smiled and said, "Please know that I am aware of the hazards." She carried with her the serenity of one who had already surrendered outcome to Providence. When her plane disappeared somewhere over the Pacific, the world mourned. Yet even in loss, her life continued to speak, a parable of courage offered to future generations.

Amelia Earhart's example still teaches that true courage is not the absence of fear but she presence of faith. She dared because she trusted, she risked because she believed, and she flew because she listened to the voice that calls each soul to rise. Her story reminds every woman that courage need not be loud to be lasting. It is found in every heart that obeys conviction despite uncertainty, in every mother who stands firm for truth, in every wife who keeps hope through trial, in every daughter who looks up and believes that she, too, was made to soar.

Reflection Questions

Where is God asking me to act in faith though fear still whispers against it?

How can my steadfastness in marriage and home strengthen the courage of those who watch me?

What lesson from a past generation reminds me that obedience is never wasted?

How might love, rather than pride, become the reason I stand firm in hard seasons?

Prayer for Courage

Lord of Mercy,

Teach me to walk without fear, for Thou art with me. Strengthen my heart to obey when comfort would persuade me to withdraw.

Let my faith become a refuge for those who dwell beneath my care. Guard my speech that it may bring peace, and guide my hands to works of quiet bravery.

When trials rise, remind me that Thy strength is made perfect in weakness. Give me the courage to keep covenant, to forgive freely, to endure with grace.

May my children learn through my life that faith is fearless because it trusts Thee. Let every act of obedience bear witness to Thy faithfulness through all generations.

In the name of Jesus Christ, Amen.

CHAPTER 27

Family Heritage: The Stories That Built Us

"ONE generation shall praise Thy works to another, and shall declare Thy mighty acts." — PSALM 145 : 4

FAMILY HERITAGE

Heritage is the soil where faith takes root. It holds the stories, prayers, and sacrifices that shaped who we are long before our names were known. Every family bears the fingerprints of God in its history, even when those prints are hidden beneath years of dust. When a woman pauses to remember where she came from, she begins to see that her story is part of something sacred, a divine continuity that runs from Eden to eternity.

To honor one's heritage is not to glorify the past, but to discern God's hand within it. It is to look back with gratitude rather than nostalgia, knowing that His providence often shines brightest in the humble lives that never made headlines. The faith of grandmothers who prayed through hardship, the loyalty of fathers who worked quietly for their children's peace, the obedience of mothers who sang hymns over sleeping infants; these are the stones upon which families are built.

The stories that built us deserve remembrance because they remind us who God has been. They reveal that every answered prayer, every redeemed failure, and every act of forgiveness contributed to the foundation we now stand upon. Forgetting them impoverishes the soul, but remembering them enriches our worship. Gratitude turns ancestry into altar, and remembrance becomes a form of praise.

Heritage calls us to humility. We are not self-made people but the continuation of promises kept by others. The faith that abides in us began as a spark in those who came before. When we trace their devotion, we find the thread of God's mercy weaving through generations, proving that no family story is too fractured for His redemption.

Heritage in Marriage

Every marriage enters a story already begun. The vows we make are not written on blank pages; they are inked upon the parchment of family legacies. Each husband and wife bring histories of both brokenness and blessing, and courage lies in allowing grace to write a new chapter. Heritage reminds a couple that their union is part of a larger covenant; one that God Himself authored long before they met.

To honor the heritage within marriage is to study how faithfulness was lived by those who came before and to redeem what was left undone. Some inherit patterns of patience and loyalty; others inherit silence or sorrow. Yet within every lineage God offers the chance to choose differently. A courageous couple takes the good that was given and forgives the rest. They do not bury the past in shame but sow it into wisdom.

When a wife remembers the heritage of devotion from those who loved steadfastly, she learns to strengthen her own home with the same steady grace. She prays for her marriage not as an isolated bond but as a link in a divine chain that stretches backward and forward. Every act of mercy within her home becomes an answer to prayers uttered by ancestors who longed for righteousness they might never see.

Marriage becomes more than companionship; it becomes the vessel through which God continues His faithfulness to a family line. When husband and wife build together with this vision, their covenant no longer feels fragile but eternal. They become stewards of a sacred trust, shaping a heritage that their children will one day remember with gratitude.

Heritage in Motherhood

A mother is the historian of the home. Through her memory and her voice, she preserves the record of God's goodness. Her stories, told again and again at the table or before bedtime, teach her children that they belong to something lasting. The tales of how their grandparents prayed, how God provided when there was little, how forgiveness healed where anger had divided; these become the curriculum of faith passed from one generation to the next.

To nurture heritage is to teach identity through gratitude. Children who know the faith of their ancestors grow roots that reach deep when storms come. They learn that their lives did not begin at birth but are part of a continuing testimony of grace. Every memory of goodness strengthens their moral spine, reminding them that the same God who sustained their family before will sustain them now. A mother's words can restore dignity to forgotten chapters. She tells her children that even the painful parts of their history are not wasted, for God redeems every story surrendered to Him. When she teaches them to honor those who came before, she also teaches them to honor themselves rightly, to see their place within God's unfolding plan.

Heritage in motherhood is not about tracing bloodlines for pride but about recognizing divine purpose. It is about showing children that they are heirs not only of genetics, but of grace. Every bedtime story of faith, every family song, every meal prepared in remembrance of God's goodness becomes a way of saying, we remember who gave us to one another.

Heritage in Sisterhood

Sisterhood thrives when women share their stories rather than compete for them. Heritage is a bond that unites across generations and across households. When women gather and recount the faithfulness of God, something eternal happens: memory becomes ministry. The younger hear what endurance sounds like, and the older see that their faith has not been forgotten.

True sisterhood refuses to let any story fade into silence. It asks questions, listens long, and celebrates what God has done in another's life. This exchange builds a living archive of courage. Each testimony strengthens the next, proving that God is the same through every age and circumstance. The shared remembrance of women keeps the faith alive when culture grows cold.

Courageous sisterhood also mends the rifts between families. It reminds women that they are all daughters within the same divine household. When they choose to honor one another's histories rather than compete for significance, unity replaces envy. Every retold story of redemption becomes an invitation to grace.

In the tapestry of womanhood, sisterhood is the thread that carries color from one generation to the next. Without it, memory fades; with it, remembrance multiplies. When women honor the heritage of others as carefully as their own, they embody the heart of Christ, who wove every lineage into the story of His redemption.

Heritage In Worship

Ultimately, all heritage returns to its Author. God is the Keeper of every lineage and the Redeemer of every name. Our family stories are not random, but instruments of His mercy. When we bring our ancestry before Him, He teaches us to see beyond earthly legacy to eternal inheritance. He reveals that the faith of our forebears was never their achievement but His grace at work within them.

To remember God's hand through generations is to worship. It is to see His patience stretched across centuries and His promises unfolding through ordinary lives. The Lord who guided Abraham, who preserved Ruth, who strengthened Mary, is the same Lord who watches over our homes today. When we recognize His authorship, pride yields to awe, and gratitude becomes our offering. Every family has seasons of failure and faith. When we place our lineage before God, He redeems what sin has written and rewrites it with mercy. In His hands, even fractured stories become vessels of grace. He takes the forgotten and calls them beloved, transforming sorrow into seed.

Heritage toward God ends in surrender. We acknowledge that the story belongs to Him alone. Our task is to remember, to give thanks, and to pass on the faith that was given to us. In doing so, we join the great chorus of generations who have declared His works one to another and found peace in His faithfulness. The stories that built us are not merely memories but instructions. They remind us that what we choose to honor today becomes the foundation our children will build upon tomorrow.

THE WIFE AND MOTHER GOD CALLS FOR THIS HOUR
FROM MY HEARTH

I have always loved a good story. Even as a child, I was drawn to tales of courage, kindness, and home, the kind that linger after the last word is spoken. I didn't yet realize that my own family carried stories just as extraordinary, waiting quietly in the roots beneath my feet. I remember my grandmother telling me that I carried sixteen percent Native Ute blood. I didn't fully understand what that meant, but I felt proud that my family had walked this land long before the Pilgrims ever arrived. Later, I would learn about the woman behind that lineage, my third greatgrandmother Ruth.

They called her Aunt Ruth, though she seemed to belong to everyone. She was the town midwife, the nurse, the sister to every mother who labored through the night. The nearest doctor was forty miles away, so Ruth became the one the town depended on. She never turned away a stranger. She fed neighbors and travelers, welcomed the local tribes into her home, and tended to the sick with a calm that steadied those around her.

Her house was always clean, her hands always busy, her heart always open. Every scrap of fabric found its way into a quilt, stitched from worn shirts and bits of wool, padded with sheep shavings when batting was scarce. Those quilts wrapped new brides and newborns alike, given as gifts for weddings and winter nights. They were more than blankets; they were testaments of love, proof that even the smallest remnants can become beauty in faithful hands.

Ruth married James on Christmas Day. Together, they raised children who followed her path of healing, nurses, doctors, and caregivers who carried her compassion forward. Her legacy taught me that history is not something distant or dusty; it is alive in the way we serve, love, and build the world around us. As I grew older, that sense of belonging deepened. I began to wonder about the families who came before Ruth, the ones who crossed oceans to worship freely, who risked everything so faith could take root in a new land. That search led me to another ancestor: my eleventh great-grandfather, William Brewster, a humble passenger on the Mayflower.

Before he ever set sail, Brewster was already a fugitive; printing Bibles and pamphlets on a press he built himself when the king sought to twist Scripture for power. His defiance made him an outlaw, but his faith made him a pilgrim. When he left England, he carried conviction across the sea. In the New World he became a pastor to the Plymouth people and printed the only Bibles they would have for many years; still on that same press, now known as the Brewster Press.

THE STORIES THAT BUILT US

From Ruth's quilts to Brewster's press, my family's story began to feel like a single tapestry, stitched with compassion, courage, and conviction. It reminded me that God's hand threads through every generation, sewing families, stories, and nations into one divine design.

Before books and screens, families told stories by memory and song. They gathered around firelight and spoke of where they came from, not for entertainment, but for endurance. They wanted their children to know who they were and Who had carried them. Today we live in a world overflowing with information yet starving for remembrance. But God still tells the truest story, one of lineage, legacy, and love.

He reminds us that where we came from matters. That our family lines are not accidents, but appointments. Each ancestor's obedience becomes the soil for our own. Each faithful choice becomes a seed for generations to come.

Your family's history is not just about where you came from; it's about Who carried you here. Every ancestor who prayed, every mother who stayed faithful, every father who stood for truth, they all sing in your blood.

So now, when I trace the names in our family line, I see more than history; I see heritage. Because their faith became my freedom. Because their courage became my inheritance. Because their God is still my God. And like Brewster and Ruth, I know my mission, to carry the truth forward. God is not distant. Our God is alive.

And His story; the story written through families, continues still, one generation at a time. We are not the first to walk this path of faith. Each generation before us has carried a measure of the promise, passing it forward through prayer, perseverance, and love. Their faith built the foundations we now stand upon, just as ours will one day become the ground beneath our children's feet.

Legacy is not kept in monuments or museums; it lives in memory and obedience. The stories that built us are not meant to end with us; they are meant to continue through us. When we honor the faith of our forebears, we join the unbroken testimony of God's covenant love, written line by line through ordinary families who believed He was faithful still.

Reflection Questions

What family story or testimony of faith most reminds me of God's presence through generations?

How can I speak of my heritage in a way that restores gratitude rather than pride?

In what ways can I redeem painful parts of my family history by surrendering them to God's mercy?

What story do I hope my children will one day tell about the faith they witnessed in our home?

Prayer for Heritage

Father of Generations,

Teach me to see Thy hand in every story that shaped my home. Help me to honor the faith of those who came before and to forgive where grace was forgotten.

Let my remembrance become worship and my gratitude become testimony. Preserve our family as a thread in Thy divine tapestry.

Guard us from arrogance, and fill us with humble thanksgiving. May every word I speak of my lineage point to Thee, the true Keeper of our name.

Let our home be a place where Thy goodness is remembered and retold.

In the name of Jesus Christ, Amen.

CHAPTER 28

Teaching Generations

"*TRAIN* up a child in the way he should go: and when he is old, he will not depart from it." — *PROVERBS 22 : 6*

TEACHING GENERATIONS

Every generation is both a harvest and a field. We gather what was planted by those before us, and we sow what others will one day reap. Teaching generations is therefore not a single moment of instruction but a lifelong ministry of remembrance. It is the sacred rhythm by which faith passes from one heart to another until the world hears again the voice of God through the living testimony of His people. The lessons that endure are not taught from pulpits alone but within homes and habits. They are carried in tone, in patience, in small obediences that shape the soul more deeply than any lecture could. When a woman chooses integrity over indulgence or prayer over panic, she writes a quiet curriculum of faith for those who watch her. She becomes an unwritten book of wisdom that her children will read long after she is gone.

To teach another generation is to believe that truth is worth remembering. It requires endurance, for hearts often learn slowly. Seeds of righteousness sometimes rest unseen beneath the soil of youth, yet God waters them faithfully. The woman who teaches generations must walk by faith, trusting that what she plants in love will bear fruit in God's appointed time.

At the heart of this calling lies loyalty, the unwavering decision to remain faithful to what is good, to uphold what is holy, and to keep speaking truth even when few seem to listen. Teaching generations is not about control but continuity, ensuring that the light entrusted to us does not grow dim before the next dawn.

Teaching Generations in Marriage

Marriage is the first classroom where love learns endurance. Within that covenant, each act of forgiveness, each word of patience, becomes a living lesson to all who behold it. The vows spoken before witnesses find their true fulfillment in daily obedience. A husband and wife who honor their promise teach that commitment is not confined to ceremony; it is renewed each morning through grace.

When a woman loves her husband faithfully through both ease and trial, she demonstrates that affection grounded in covenant outlasts the winds of circumstance. Her consistency tells her family that love is not merely emotion but devotion. Even her moments of silence can speak when they are filled with prayer instead of resentment. Her gentleness teaches strength more powerfully than her argument ever could.

Teaching through marriage requires humility. It means confessing quickly, forgiving fully, and choosing unity over pride. The children who grow within such a home learn that peace is not accidental but cultivated. They see that honor is not demanded but earned through service. They come to believe that love is safest when it is anchored in truth.

When two souls keep covenant under God, their faithfulness becomes a heritage. Each small act of perseverance becomes another stone in the foundation for those who will follow. The courage to remain tender in the face of hardship becomes a testimony that will instruct generations long after their voices fall silent.

Teaching Generations in Motherhood

A mother preaches her most persuasive sermons without words. Every meal she prepares, every wound she tends, every prayer she whispers becomes a verse of faith written into the hearts of her children. They may forget her advice, but they will not forget her example. In her steadfastness they come to understand what holiness looks like in human form.

To teach through motherhood is to accept a sacred patience. The results cannot be measured in days but in decades. The lessons she imparts must often be entrusted to God's timing. When she chooses consistency over comfort, she teaches endurance; when she answers with gentleness, she teaches grace. The tone of her correction and the depth of her forgiveness instruct more than any rule or routine.

Her motherhood also reaches beyond her own household. The influence of a godly woman spills into every relationship she touches. When she nurtures children not her own or offers counsel to a younger mother, she extends the circle of learning that defines Christian womanhood. Her life becomes a conduit of truth from one soul to another.

Above all, a mother's teaching is intercession. She teaches faith by practicing it. Her children learn dependence upon God by watching her pray, and they learn confidence in His care by seeing her rest. Though time and distance may separate them, her faith becomes a living inheritance that no circumstance can erase.

Teaching Generations in Sisterhood

Among women, the chain of teaching is both delicate and enduring. Older women carry the wisdom of experience; younger women carry the eagerness of discovery. When humility binds the two together, the beauty of discipleship unfolds. Each gives what the other needs, and both are strengthened.

Sisterhood becomes holy when women choose to share truth instead of comparison. To listen with patience, to speak with kindness, to correct with compassion, these are the arts of spiritual mentorship. The woman who teaches another to love her home, to honor her husband, and to raise her children in faith is fulfilling one of Scripture's oldest commands. Her counsel becomes a bridge across generations, keeping the faith alive through relationship.

Teaching in sisterhood also guards against isolation. No woman was meant to journey alone. When one falters, another steadies her; when one rejoices, another amplifies her joy. The circle of faithful women becomes a sanctuary where burdens are shared and hope renewed. Such fellowship is not friendship alone; it is a continuation of divine design. When women honor the generations before them and invest in those who follow, they weave a tapestry of loyalty and love that reflects heaven's order. In every conversation guided by grace, in every moment of mutual prayer, they proclaim that God's wisdom is meant to be lived together, not burdened alone.

Teaching Generations Toward God

All true teaching is participation in the work of God. He does not ask us to invent wisdom but to transmit it. The woman who teaches another in the ways of faith becomes an instrument through whom divine truth continues its journey through time. Her calling is not to preserve ideas but to cultivate living faith in those who follow.

Teaching toward God begins with intimacy. Before she can lead anyone to prayer, she must have walked the path herself. Instruction becomes powerful only when it flows from communion. The one who has wrestled with doubt and found peace, who has labored in prayer and learned stillness, speaks with authority born of experience. Her words carry warmth because they have been tested by obedience.

The goal of this teaching is not information, but transformation. To teach another to serve, to forgive, or to rejoice in trial is to invite them into the likeness of Christ. Every act of discipleship is an act of worship, for it magnifies the goodness of the Teacher Himself. Throughout her life, the faithful woman declares that wisdom is not mastered through intellect but revealed through love.

Teaching toward God also requires vision. It looks beyond immediate results to eternal impact. The lessons she imparts today may not bear fruit until she is long gone, yet she trusts that God multiplies every seed. Her patience becomes part of His providence. The classroom of her life extends far beyond her lifetime, reaching descendants she will never meet.

When a woman teaches in this way, she becomes a living link in the chain of redemption. Her obedience joins the work of prophets, apostles, and mothers of faith who carried the truth before her. Each generation continues the great dialogue between heaven and earth; listening, learning, and leading others toward the heart of God. Every lesson of faith is a seed of loyalty. When planted in love and watered by obedience, it grows into a harvest that nourishes generations to come.

THE WIFE AND MOTHER GOD CALLS FOR THIS HOUR

RUTH

"INTREAT me not to leave thee, or to return from following after thee." — RUTH 1 : 16

In the days when judges ruled Israel, famine drove a family from Bethlehem to the foreign fields of Moab. There Elimelech and Naomi raised their two sons, who later married Moabite women, Orpah and Ruth. When famine turned to grief and death claimed the men, three widows remained; three women bound by sorrow and uncertain hope. Naomi, weary and heartsick, resolved to return home. She urged her daughters-in-law to remain among their own people, to seek new lives and new husbands. Orpah, with tears, kissed her mother-in-law farewell. But Ruth clung to Naomi with a love stronger than fear and spoke words that would echo through centuries: "Whither thou goest, I will go; thy people shall be my people, and thy God my God."

That pledge was more than affection; it was faith. Ruth turned her back on her homeland, her idols, and her certainty of provision. She chose instead the uncertain road of obedience, trusting the character of the God she had only glimpsed through Naomi's witness. The journey back to Bethlehem was long and poor. The two widows arrived with little more than each other. Yet in Ruth's steadfast spirit, Naomi glimpsed the kindness of God she had thought forgotten.

To sustain them, Ruth rose early each morning to glean in the fields after the reapers. She gathered the scattered grain with humble diligence, a foreigner among the people of Israel. Her gentleness and labor did not go unnoticed. Boaz, a man of integrity and distant relative of Naomi, observed her faithfulness. He blessed her in the name of the Lord and commanded that she be protected and provided for. Ruth's heart overflowed with gratitude, not merely for Boaz's kindness but for God's providence that had guided her steps to that field. When Naomi learned whose field Ruth had entered, hope stirred anew. She recognized the hand of the Redeemer drawing near. Guided by Naomi's counsel, Ruth approached Boaz in humility, seeking redemption according to the law of kinship. Her request was not presumption but trust. She rested at the feet of grace, believing that God could restore what loss had taken.

THE LOYALTY OF LOVE

Boaz honored her virtue, declaring that all Bethlehem knew her to be a woman of excellence. In time, he redeemed both Ruth and the inheritance of Elimelech. Their union brought forth a son named Obed, the grandfather of David and ancestor of Christ. Thus, the loyalty of one foreign widow became the lineage through which salvation entered the world.

Ruth's story is more than a romance; it is a revelation. It shows that God weaves outsiders into His covenant when hearts choose faith over fear. Her loyalty to Naomi reflected divine compassion; her humility before Boaz mirrored the soul's posture before the Redeemer. Through her life, the Lord displayed that redemption is born not of status but of steadfast love.

The story of Ruth teaches every generation that faithfulness in the smallest acts, harvesting in humility, caring for the aged, choosing righteousness when no one sees, builds legacies that eternity remembers. Her courage turned famine into fruitfulness, her obedience turned despair into delight, and her name stands among those who trusted God enough to begin again. Ruth's loyalty did not only preserve Naomi's household; it prepared the way for the coming of Christ, the true Redeemer who gathers the outcast and crowns the faithful with everlasting mercy.

Reflection Questions

What truths or habits of faith am I intentionally sowing for the next generation to inherit?

How can my daily example speak more clearly than my instruction?

What lessons from my own upbringing reveal God's faithfulness that I might now pass forward?

In what ways can I make my home a living classroom of prayer, gratitude, and grace?

Prayer for Teaching Generations

Father of Light,

Teach me to walk before Thee in truth so that others may find the path by my footsteps. Let my words be seasoned with grace and my actions guided by wisdom.

Grant me patience to teach what is right and humility to learn what I do not yet know. Help me to build within my home a legacy of peace and praise.

Forgive my failures and redeem my example for the sake of those who follow. Let the faith that lives in me become the inheritance of my children's children.

May every generation who remembers our name see Thy mercy in our story.

In the name of Jesus Christ, Amen.

The Loyalty of Love and chapter 28

_____
_____
_____
_____
_____
_____
_____
_____
_____
_____
_____
_____
_____
_____
_____
_____
_____
_____
_____
_____
_____
_____
_____
_____
_____
_____
_____
_____
_____
_____

CHAPTER 29

Legacy & Inheritance

"ᴋɴᴏᴡ therefore that the Lord thy God, he is God, the faithful God, which keepeth covenant and mercy with them that love him and keep his commandments to a thousand generations." — ᴅᴇᴜᴛᴇʀᴏɴᴏᴍʏ 7 : 9

LEGACY & INHERITANCE

Every home writes a record. Every word spoken, every act forgiven, every prayer whispered in secret becomes part of a living inheritance. The legacy of a woman is not measured in possessions but in promises kept. It is the unseen covenant between generations; the vow that love will not end with her, that faith will not fade, that mercy will not stop where her hands grow weary.

To live with legacy in mind is to see time as a sacred trust. It is to believe that what is formed in the heart of one mother may awaken in the heart of a great-grandchild yet unborn. True inheritance is not left in will or estate but in worship and example. The faithful woman builds with eternal materials: truth, compassion, and prayer. Her home becomes both altar and ark; an offering before heaven and a vessel through which God's promises continue their journey.

When the Lord speaks of generations, He is speaking of story. He writes His mercy across family lines, asking each household to keep the record of His faithfulness alive. To remember is to renew. The woman who remembers His goodness signs her name upon the long covenant of grace. She becomes a keeper of continuity; a bridge between what has been redeemed and what will be restored.

Legacy is not pride in the past but partnership in the promise. It is the assurance that what God begins, He continues through those who love Him. The inheritance of faith is not something we store away; it is something we steward daily. It grows each time we choose forgiveness over resentment, gratitude over complaint, prayer over fear. These choices become seeds of covenant that outlive the hands that sow them.

Legacy in Marriage

Marriage is the first covenant of legacy, for it reflects the eternal faithfulness of God to His people. Every vow exchanged becomes part of the family's written testimony. The way a husband and wife honor one another, especially in unseen moments, sets the tone for generations. Their patience teaches more than their success. Their unity under trial preaches more than their comfort ever could.

Legacy within marriage is not secured by romance but by reverence. When a wife keeps her word in small things, she proves that love can be trusted. When she listens with kindness and responds with grace, she teaches her children that covenant is not sentiment but stewardship. The quiet decisions; speaking gently, forgiving quickly, praying together; form the moral architecture of the household.

Every promise fulfilled between husband and wife becomes a living echo of God's faithfulness. To remain steadfast in hardship is to testify that vows are holy, not habitual. The reverent marriage becomes a lighthouse to those adrift, a reminder that the love we inherit from God is meant to be given again.

A wife who builds with legacy in mind sees her home as sacred trust. She tends not only to harmony but to memory. Her tenderness becomes tradition; her steadfastness, foundation. Long after her name is forgotten, the peace she cultivated continues to teach. Her marriage becomes part of the great covenant story; an enduring witness that love, once consecrated, is never lost.

Legacy in Motherhood

Motherhood is the art of planting what eternity will harvest. The work is slow and unseen, yet its fruit lasts forever. Each prayer whispered over a child, each correction given in patience, each word of Scripture taught with love becomes a line written in the book of generations.

The mother who thinks generationally does not despair over present struggle. She knows her labor is holy because it reaches beyond her own lifetime. She teaches her children that the promises of God are not relics but living inheritance. Every story of His deliverance, every testimony of His provision becomes a thread binding them to truth. Her legacy is not simply that she raised children, but that she raised worshipers who will raise worshipers after them.

This inheritance cannot be bought or replaced. It is passed heart to heart through example. When a mother forgives quickly, she teaches repentance. When she rejoices over small mercies, she teaches gratitude. When she trusts in difficulty, she teaches faith. These daily lessons become a covenant of character that outlasts any earthly possession.

Motherhood, lived in covenant, is an altar of remembrance. Every sacrifice, of sleep, of comfort, of ambition, becomes part of a holy record. The children of such a mother may one day wander, but they will never forget the sound of her prayers. God remembers those prayers too, and He keeps covenant and mercy with her to a thousand generations.

Legacy in Sisterhood

No covenant stands alone. Every woman's faith strengthens another's, every testimony builds the record of collective memory. The sisterhood of believers is itself an inheritance; a lineage of holy women whose reverence sustains the Church through centuries. When one woman encourages another to keep believing, she becomes part of a spiritual genealogy that stretches back to the cross.

Legacy in sisterhood is carried through words that build, not break. When women honor each other's callings, they protect the sacred trust of unity. To celebrate another's gift is to magnify the Giver. The humble sister is a bridge between hearts, helping others remember that their labor is not forgotten by God. Her kindness is a covenant of its own, written in invisible ink upon the soul.

The inheritance of sisterhood is not found in shared circumstance but in shared faith. Across time and culture, women have knelt, prayed, and persevered together. Their prayers form a living chain of remembrance. To join that chain is to agree that holiness is best preserved in community. Every act of compassion strengthens the structure of the covenant home; the collective dwelling of God's daughters.

When women speak truth in love and carry one another's burdens, they renew the vow of sisterhood that Christ Himself established. In this fellowship of grace, legacy multiplies. One woman's obedience becomes another's encouragement. One generation's perseverance becomes another's peace. Together, they keep the record of His mercy alive.

Legacy Toward God

The final inheritance is not what we leave behind but what we return. Everything entrusted to us; time, family, gifts, influence, is meant to be offered back in worship. The woman who lives in covenant understands that she owns nothing but gratitude. Her legacy toward God is not in grandeur but in faithfulness.

When she bows in prayer, she is signing her name upon heaven's record. When she forgives, she renews the vow of grace. When she gives generously, she continues the pattern of divine provision. Her every act of love is a form of remembrance, a living thank offering to the One who first loved her. The inheritance she receives from God is peace. It is the knowledge that her story, its joys, its sorrows, its ordinary days, has been gathered into the great narrative of redemption. Nothing offered in sincerity is ever lost. The cup of water given, the word of truth spoken, the small kindness extended; all are remembered by the Faithful God who keeps covenant forever.

To live with such awareness is to walk in worship. It is to see every moment as a renewal of promise, every sunrise as a reminder that His mercy is new, and every night as another seal of His faithfulness. The woman who trusts Him leaves an inheritance of light. Her family learns not merely how to pray but why; to remember.

Legacy is not the closing of a story but the continuation of it. The covenant begun in one heart moves quietly into the next, carried by love, sealed by faith, and sustained by the mercy of God to a thousand generations.

THE WIFE AND MOTHER GOD CALLS FOR THIS HOUR

FROM MY HEARTH

Some prayers are answered in a lifetime. Others take generations to unfold. I have seen the fruit of faith that began long before I was born; faith that crossed oceans, endured loss, and believed in a promise it would never see fulfilled.

One of those prayers was carried by my thirteenth great-grandmother, Mrs. James Chilton, a woman of quiet courage whose name I once read only in history books but have since come to know as family. She boarded the Mayflower beside her husband and their young daughter, Mary, with a prayer that her family might worship God freely in a land untouched by tyranny. She dreamed of a world where her daughter could lift her hands to heaven without fear of a king's decree.

The journey across the Atlantic was brutal; storm after storm beating against the ship, masts breaking, provisions running thin. The passengers prayed through the nights as the winds howled, and still they pressed on. By the time they reached the new world, they had crossed more than an ocean. They had crossed the line between oppression and freedom, between faith imprisoned and faith alive.

But Mrs. Chilton would not live to see that freedom take root. The first winter at Plymouth was merciless. Food was scarce, shelter barely held, and sickness swept through the camp. History tells that she died before spring, but I believe her last breath was also her last offering; a sacrifice that secured life for her daughter. When she had only enough cornmeal for one, she gave it to Mary. She gave her portion of life so that the promise could continue.

She knew what many of us are still learning: that living comfortably under tyranny is no life at all, and living freely in discomfort is worth everything. She gave what she could so her child could live in liberty; so that generations not yet born, including mine, could worship the God she loved without fear.

I think about her sometimes when I pray for my own children. My prayers are different in form but not in spirit. She prayed for a land of freedom; I pray for hearts that remain free. She faced the tyranny of kings; we face the tyranny of culture. Her storms were made of wind and sea; ours are of noise and distraction. But the God who heard her prayer is the same God who hears mine.

GENERATIONAL PRAYERS

When I look at my children bowing their heads in prayer, I realize that Mrs. Chilton's faith still lives; it flows through our veins like inheritance. Her obedience planted a seed that has bloomed for more than four hundred years. I am the answer to her prayer. My children are, too. The same God who brought her safely across the sea has carried our family through centuries of change, war, and trial, and still His promise remains.

Sometimes I wonder if she knew, as she lay down that last night in the bitter cold, that her prayer would echo this far. Did she imagine that one day her descendants would live in a country her courage helped build? Did she know that her surrender would become a story of redemption retold by her children's children? Perhaps not. But God knew. And His promises never expire.

Her faith reminds me that our prayers do not end with us. They become part of a lineage of hope, written into the lives of those who follow. Every whispered petition, every tear shed in trust, becomes a thread in God's tapestry of mercy. The freedom I enjoy today was once just a mother's plea in the dark; a prayer that her daughter might live and worship freely. That prayer crossed an ocean, survived a storm, and outlived its author. It became a covenant that still stands.

And so, when I kneel to pray for my family, I pray as she once did: that my children will know the God who carried us this far, that they will love truth more than comfort, and that their lives will be spent for something eternal. Because the prayers of one faithful woman made me free. And by God's grace, the prayers of another will keep our freedom alive.

The faith that carried our ancestors still calls to us now. Their prayers became the soil beneath our feet, and our obedience will one day become the ground beneath our children's. We are living answers to petitions whispered long before we arrived, and our lives will, in turn, become God's answer to generations yet unborn.

Legacy is not a story of the past; it is a living covenant between God and His people. Every act of faith, every prayer spoken in trust, becomes another thread in the tapestry of redemption. The promise does not end; it continues, line by line, heart by heart, as His mercy stretches from generation to generation.

Reflection Questions

What spiritual inheritance am I cultivating in my home that will outlast me?

How can I ensure that my words and habits reflect the faithfulness I hope to leave behind?

Which promises of God do I want my children and sisters in faith to remember most?

How can I live each day as though it is part of a vow written for generations yet to come?

Prayer for Legacy & Inheritance

Faithful God,

Thou who keepest covenant and mercy to a thousand generations, Teach me to live with eternity in mind. Let my love record Thy goodness and my obedience reflect Thy grace.

Write Thy faithfulness upon the heart of my home. Make my marriage steadfast, my motherhood fruitful, and my friendships holy.

Guard the generations that follow with the same mercy that has guarded me. When my voice grows still, let the praise I have offered continue in theirs.

Seal within our family the remembrance of Thee, That our story may testify to Thy faithfulness forever.

In the name of Jesus Christ, Amen.

Generational Prayers and Chapter 29

FROM GENERATION TO GENERATION

*"LET this be written for a future generation,
that a people not yet created may praise the Lord."* -PSALM 102:18

The Wife and Mother God Calls for This Hour
FROM MY HEARTH TO YOURS

From the beginning, God made families. He spoke the world into being, formed man from the dust, and then said it was not good for him to be alone. Out of that sacred union came the first home, the first promise, and the first covenant. Family was never an afterthought; it was God's design for how heaven would touch the earth.

Every nation begins with a household. Every legacy begins with a name. When God makes families, He is also shaping the soul of nations. What begins in our living rooms becomes the culture of a people. What is whispered in prayer around our tables becomes the strength of a country.

Your family's history is American history. The courage of our ancestors, the sacrifices they made, the prayers they prayed; all of it flows into the freedoms we now enjoy. They crossed oceans, faced tyrants, buried their dead in frozen ground, and still they sang hymns of hope. They built more than colonies and towns; they built a covenant, trusting that liberty was worth the cost.

Now it is our turn.

It is our time not only to remember those who came before us, but to carry their legacy forward; to live so that our children have something sacred to continue, and a country still worth keeping. The freedoms we enjoy were bought and paid for with the lives and liberty of those who believed that faith was stronger than fear and that truth was worth defending.

Let us not be the generation that forgets. Let us be the generation that restores, who teach our sons and daughters that freedom is not inherited by blood alone, but by belief. That our blessings demand stewardship. That the covenant of faith and family must be renewed in every home before it can be restored in any nation.

When I think of the women who came before me; Ruth the midwife, Mrs. Chilton on the Mayflower, the mothers who prayed through wars and winters; I see the

ONE GENERATION TO THE NEXT

pattern of God's faithfulness. They lived as though their obedience mattered for the next hundred years, and it did. Their faith became my freedom.

And so it is with us.

Our prayers today are the foundations of tomorrow's history. The way we love our husbands, nurture our children, and honor God in our homes will ripple through generations we may never meet. Every meal shared in gratitude, every truth spoken in grace, every act of courage born from conviction; it all becomes part of the story He is still writing through His people.

We are heirs of a holy legacy. The same God who led the pilgrims across the sea, who strengthened the patriots on the field, who comforted mothers waiting at the window, is still leading us now. His covenant endures. His mercy continues from generation to generation.

So we stand where they once stood; between promise and responsibility, between faith remembered and faith renewed; and we choose to keep the light burning.

Because God makes families.

And families make nations.

May the story of your home become part of the story of His faithfulness; and may those who come after you rise and call you blessed.

The Wife and Mother God Calls for This Hour

A CLOSING PRAYER

Father of Generations,

Thank You for the story You have written through our families.
   for the faith that crossed oceans, the courage that built homes, and the grace that still holds us today.

Teach us to honor what has been entrusted to us.
     Let the altars built by our ancestors remind us that Your promises never fail.
     Make our homes strong in truth, gentle in mercy, and steadfast in the covenant of faith and family.

May our children inherit not only our name, but our devotion to You.
     May our prayers become the foundations of their freedom,
     and may our obedience become the testimony of Your goodness.

Lord, let every house that bears Your name shine as a light to the nation You have blessed.
     Renew in us the courage to protect liberty, to preserve truth,
     and to live as families who remember that You alone are the Giver of every good thing.

And, Lord, strengthen the women who keep these homes—steady their hearts, renew their courage, and let them walk in the calling You have placed upon their generation.

From our hearths to the heart of this country, let Your covenant continue,
   from generation to generation, until the story You began is complete in Christ.

In the name of Jesus Christ, Amen.

A CLOSING PRAYER AND FROM GENERATION TO GENERATION

www.ingramcontent.com/pod-product-compliance
Lightning Source LLC
Chambersburg PA
CBHW051324110526
44582CB00004B/97